digging deeper

4 THE TWENTIETH CENTURY WORLD

ALAN BROOKS-TYREMAN   JANE SHUTER   KATE SMITH

Heinemann

Heinemann Educational Publishers
Halley Court, Jordan Hill, Oxford, OX2 8EJ
a division of Reed Educational & Professional Publishing Ltd
Heinemann is a registered trademark of Reed Educational & Professional Publishing Ltd

OXFORD MELBOURNE AUCKLAND
JOHANNESBURG BLANTYRE GABORONE
IBADAN PORTSMOUTH NH (USA) CHICAGO

© Heinemann Educational Publishers 2000

Copyright notice

All rights reserved. No part of this publication may be reproduced in any material form (including photocopying or storing it in any medium by electronic means and whether or not transiently or incidentally to some other use of this publication) without the prior written permission of the copyright owner, except in accordance with the provisions of the Copyright, Designs and Patents Act 1988 or under the terms of a licence issued by the Copyright Licensing Agency Ltd, 90 Tottenham Court Road, London W1P 0LP. Applications for the copyright owner's written permission to reproduce any part of this publication should be addressed to the publisher.

First published 2000

ISBN 0 435 32772 0

02 01 00
10 9 8 7 6 5 4 3 2 1

Designed and produced by Gecko Limited, Bicester, Oxon

Original illustrations © Heinemann Educational Publishers 2000

Illustrated by Mike Spoor and Geoff Ward

Printed and bound in Spain by Mateu Cromo

Photographic acknowledgements

The authors and publishers would like to thank the following for permission to reproduce photographs:

Associated Press: 31, 48, Max Nash: 14; BFI: 57; the art archive: 11; Ronald Grant Archive: 24; Robert Harding: 58, 60; Hulton Getty: 5, 8, 19, 26, 33, 39, 42, 47, 53; Imperial War Museum: 44, 51; David King: 55; London Transport Museum: 21; NASA: 61; Panstowowe Museum, Poland: 34; Ursula Koscielniak: 35; Punch Library: 4, 6; Quadrant: 40; Rex Features Ltd: 38; Retna, Anthony Saint-James: 62; US Holocaust Memorial Museum: 37; Weiner Library: 13

Picture research by Helen Reilly

Cover photograph © AKG London.

Written sources acknowledgements

The authors and publishers gratefully acknowledge the following publications from which written sources in the book are drawn. In some sources the wording or sentence has been simplified.

Primo Levi, *The Truce, a Survivor's Journey Home from Auschwitz*, The Bodley Head, Orion Press, 1965: 12A

George Orwell, *1984*, The Bodley Head, 1948: 55G

M. Phillips & T. Phillips, *Windrush, the Irresistible Rise of Multi-Racial Britain*, Harper Collins, 1998: 20A–E

H. B. C. Pollard, *The Story of Ypres*, Robert M. McBride and Co., 1917: 10F

Gena Turgel, *I Light a Candle*, Valentine Mitchell, 1987: 12B, 13C, D,14F

R. Westall & J. Simkin, *Comrades in Arms*, Tressell, 1988: 10D

The publishers have made every effort to trace the copyright holders, but if they have inadvertently overlooked any, they will be pleased to make the necessary arrangements at the first opportunity.

CONTENTS

HISTORICAL SKILLS

Investigating an issue through sources. Did the Suffragettes help win the vote for women? . . .4
Using eye-witness sources. The First World War – written accounts from the trenches 8
Learning from eye-witnesses. Liberating the concentration camps .12
Assessing the evidence. Was the bombing of Hiroshima and Nagasaki justified? 15
Understanding short-term causes. The development of a multi-cultural society 19

DIGGING DEEPER

Massacre at Amritsar 22
Chinese women – bound to the home? 26
Exploding rats – the gadgets of the SOE 28
'Got any gum, chum?' – US troops in Britain 30
Keeping each other going 34
Adolf Eichmann: Nazi on the run 36
The swinging 60s 38

THEMES

Warfare in the twentieth century 42
Controlling the hearts and minds of the people: Propaganda in the twentieth century . . .50
Taking time out 56
Glossary 63

Investigating an issue through sources

Did the Suffragettes help win the vote for women?

No vote

During the nineteenth century the right to vote in general elections in Britain had been extended to include almost all adult males. But, although women could vote in elections for their local council, they had no say in who should be elected as a Member of Parliament and, therefore, no say in which party formed the government.

As early as 1851 one woman campaigner had complained that it was not justifiable that 'one half of the human race should pass through life in a state of enforced inferiority, when the only reason that can be given is that men like it'. In 1867 one MP had tried to persuade Parliament to pass a law extending the vote to women, but his proposal was outvoted.

The campaign begins

In 1897 a group of women set up the National Union of Women's Suffrage Societies to try to win suffrage (the right to vote) for women. This group believed in peaceful protest, such as organising petitions and writing letters to MPs. Soon some women decided that more **militant** action was needed. In 1903, Emmeline Pankhurst and her daughters Sylvia and Christabel set up the Women's Social and Political Union. The WSPU believed in 'deeds, not words' and gained publicity by extreme measures, such as smashing shop windows, **arson**, and stone throwing. One woman, Emily Wilding Davison, even gave up her life when she was killed at the **Derby** in 1913. She ran on to the course during the race and tried to stop a horse which belonged to the king.

Source A

A cartoon from a magazine published in 1906. At this time Britain was governed by the Liberal Party.

SOURCE B

Emily Wilding Davison.

Divided opinions

The actions of these 'Suffragettes' (as they became known) caused quite a stir. Their activities were reported in the newspapers and there was great debate about the wisdom of their actions. Suffragette supporters said that they were doing an excellent job in publicising 'the cause'. Opponents said that they were showing women to be irresponsible and not deserving of the vote on the same terms as men. One group of women even started the Women's Anti-Suffrage League opposing votes for women. Not surprisingly there was also a Men's League for Opposing Women's Suffrage.

SOURCE C

On 8 October 1909 Christabel Pankhurst and I were on our way to Newcastle. I had made up my mind that I was going to throw a stone. We went to the Haymarket where the car with Lloyd George would probably pass. As the motor appeared I stepped out into the road and shouted:

'How can you, when you say you back the woman's cause, stay in a government which refuses them the vote and is persecuting them for it?'

Then I threw the stone at the car, aiming low to avoid injuring the chauffeur or passengers.

Lady Constance Lytton, a well known Suffragette, describing her first violent act on behalf of the campaign to win votes for women. As a result of this incident Lady Lytton was arrested and fined. She refused to pay the fine, was sent to prison and went on hunger strike.

SOURCE D

Failure to understand that man is the master, and why, is at the root of the suffrage movement. Suffragettes ignore man's superior strength and they ignore man's superior mind, so come to believe that they can think as well as men.

An extract from a book written by Sir A.E. Wright in 1913.

SOURCE E

Hasn't Mrs Pankhurst the sense to see that the very worst way of campaigning for the vote is to try to intimidate or blackmail a man into giving her what he would gladly give her otherwise?

David Lloyd George speaking in 1913, after a group of Suffragettes had carried out a bomb attack on his house.

The war

When the First World War broke out in 1914, the Suffragettes called off their campaign and instead launched themselves into war work. Over 1000 imprisoned Suffragettes were released. With so many men away fighting, there was plenty of work for women to do. Hundreds of thousands of them worked in factories turning out guns, artillery shells and equipment. Women took over the jobs of train drivers, office clerks, agricultural labourers and many others. Their work won them enormous respect from many men who had previously seen women as second class citizens.

The vote won

In 1917 the government began drawing up a list of voters for a General Election to be held at the end of the war. In order to vote men had to have lived at the same address for at least a year. This meant that thousands of soldiers had lost their right to vote, so a new law had to be introduced. The government decided that in this law women should also be given the vote. On 10 January 1918 Parliament passed the Representation of the People Act giving the vote to men aged over 21 and women aged over 30 years of age.

Had the Suffragettes won women the vote or would it have happened anyway? Your task is to study the sources and reach a decision.

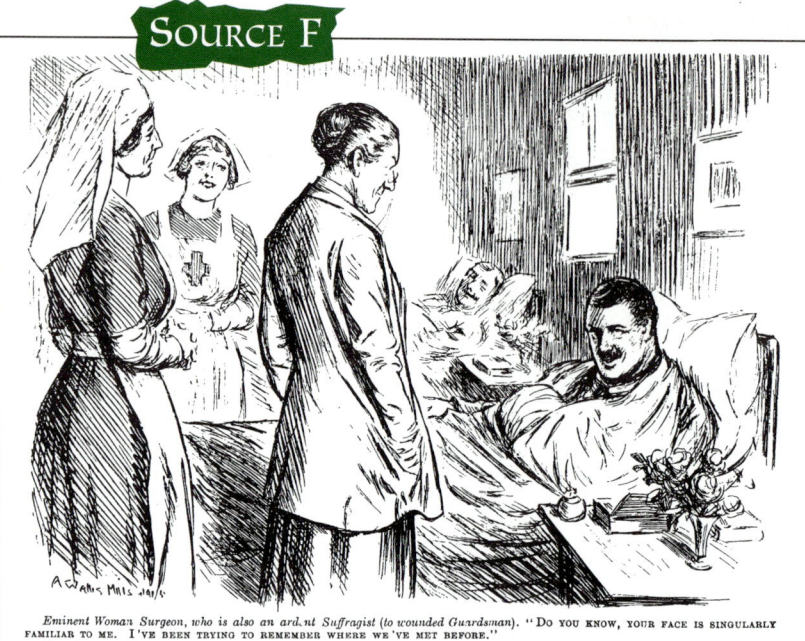

Source F

Eminent Woman Surgeon, who is also an ardent Suffragist (to wounded Guardsman). "DO YOU KNOW, YOUR FACE IS SINGULARLY FAMILIAR TO ME. I'VE BEEN TRYING TO REMEMBER WHERE WE'VE MET BEFORE."
Guardsman. "WELL, MUM, BYGONES BE BYGONES. I WAS A POLICE CONSTABLE."

A cartoon from 1915. It was published in the same magazine as the cartoon in Source A.

Source G

It is difficult to know whether violence helped or hindered the cause. Historians tend to conclude that the violence made Prime Minister Asquith's opposition to votes for women easier, and life for supporters such as Lloyd George more difficult. But it cannot be blamed for women's failure to gain the vote before the war. When Parliament passed a Bill giving women the vote in 1918, it did so not only because women had contributed valiantly to the war effort, but also because the Suffragettes had ensured that the issue could not be ignored.

A recent historian commenting on the role of the Suffragettes in winning the vote for women.

SOURCE H

I do not believe that we would have won the vote when we did if it had not been necessary for the government to act to make sure that all the men who had served their country could still vote. By sheer necessity the government was forced to change the law dealing with the whole voting issue.

Millicent Fawcett, a leading Suffragette, writing about women and the vote in a book published in 1922.

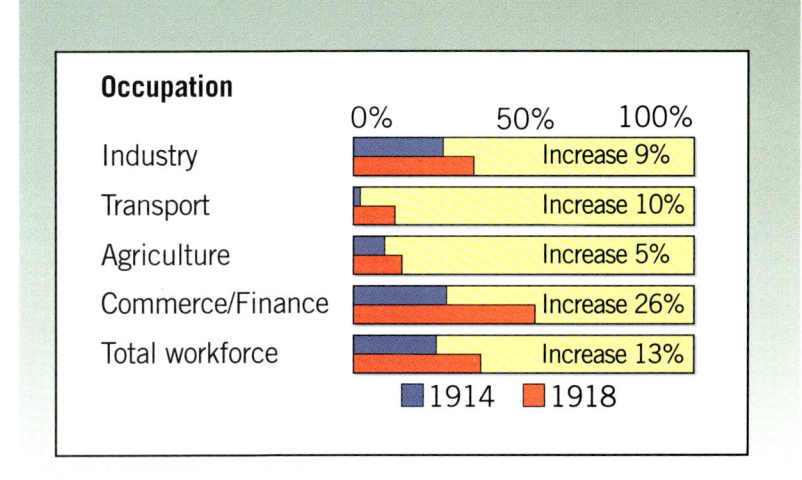

Occupation	1914 / 1918	Change
Industry		Increase 9%
Transport		Increase 10%
Agriculture		Increase 5%
Commerce/Finance		Increase 26%
Total workforce		Increase 13%

Women as a percentage of the workforce in Britain in 1914 and 1918.

Work it out!

1 Study Source A.

What do you think the cartoonist was trying to say?

2 Study Source C.

Do you agree that Lady Constance Lytton was unlikely to achieve anything by throwing stones, so her action was pointless? Explain your answer.

3 Study Sources D and E.

Do you think that what is said in these two sources proves that the Suffragettes had achieved little by 1913? Explain your answer.

4 Study the chart on this page.

   a What does it tell us about the work of women in the war?

   b What else would you need to know before you could say that this source gave you a good picture of how womens' lives changed as a result of the war?

5 Study Source F.

Do you think this cartoonist supported or opposed the Suffragettes? Explain your answer.

6 Study Sources G and H.

Do these sources suggest that the Suffragettes were responsible for helping women to win the vote? Explain your answer.

7 Write a short speech (about 200 words) either praising or condemning the Suffragettes. Remember to use the information on these pages to support your answer.

Using eye-witness sources

The First World War – written accounts from the trenches

In 1914 both sides were confident that the war would be fought between quick-moving armies and that 'it would all be over by Christmas'. At the beginning of 1915, however, the armies had failed to advance and millions of soldiers were dug into strong positions in trenches, facing the enemy across **No Man's Land**. Over 600 kilometres of trenches stretched from the Channel coast in Belgium to the mountains of Switzerland and were known as the Western Front. Both sides tried in vain to push the enemy back, the casualties were enormous, and the war became a war of **stalemate**.

Writers of the First World War

Many letters, reminiscences, journals, newspaper reports and songs remain from the war. All these are primary sources, but we have to remember that letters from soldiers home were **censored**, and people at home were urged to be cheerful and keep back depressing news. Newspaper journalists also wrote reports without really understanding life at the front.

There are many poems about the First World War. Most of them are written by soldiers who fought in the trenches, and not only do they describe what life in the trenches was like, but they tell us what the poets thought about the meaning and the purpose of war.

Two famous poets

Siegfried Sassoon and Wilfred Owen both fought in the First World War. Sassoon was a novelist and poet who wrote a great deal about the war. He was posted to France with the Royal Welsh Fusiliers in 1915, and was nicknamed 'Mad Jack' for his bravery and awarded the MC. Wounded in 1917, he suffered a reaction against the war while recovering in England, and made a public statement defying military authority because he believed that 'the war is being deliberately prolonged by those who have the power to end it'. He was not **court-martialled**, however, as he was thought to be suffering from shell shock, and he fought again in 1918. He died in 1967.

Wilfred Owen (1893-1918) fought in the trenches on the Western Front and was awarded the Military Cross. He was killed one week before the war ended.

Sassoon and Owen met in the summer of 1917 in Scotland. The young Owen showed some of his poems to Sassoon who encouraged him and recommended changes. Both men wrote what they felt about war. Amongst the many unfinished jotting and poems in Owen's papers were the lines 'All the poet can do today is warn. That is why true poets must be truthful'.

Wilfred Owen photographed in 1916 by John Gunston.

Source A

It was a wet night, and I'd been out with the wiring party (trenches were 'protected' with barbed wire) from ten till twelve. Lugging rolls of concertina wire along a narrow trench swilling with mud and water wasn't much fun. Stumbling with it over shell holes was worse. Now and again, I had to whack a rat running along the wall.

Back in the main trench, I stood to watch the sky whitening. Sad and blighted the country emerged. I could see the ruined village below the hill and the leafless trees; there seemed no comfort left in life. My steel hat was heavy on my head.

And here I was, staring across at the enemy I'd never seen. Without knowing why, I remembered that it was Easter Sunday, standing in that dismal ditch, I could find no understanding in the thought that Christ was risen.

An extract from Siegfried Sassoon's autobiography.

Source B

'O Jesus Christ' one fellow sighed.

And kneeled and bowed tho' not in prayer and died.

And the bullets sang 'In Vain',

Big Guns guffawed 'In Vain'.

'Last Words' by Wilfred Owen.

Source C

'Good morning: good morning!' the General said

When we met him last week on our way to the line.

Now the soldiers he smiled at are most of 'em dead,

And we're cursing his staff for incompetent swine.

'He's a cheery old card' grunted Harry to Jack

As they slogged up to Arras with rifle and pack.

But he did for them both by his plan of attack.

'The General' by Siegfried Sassoon.

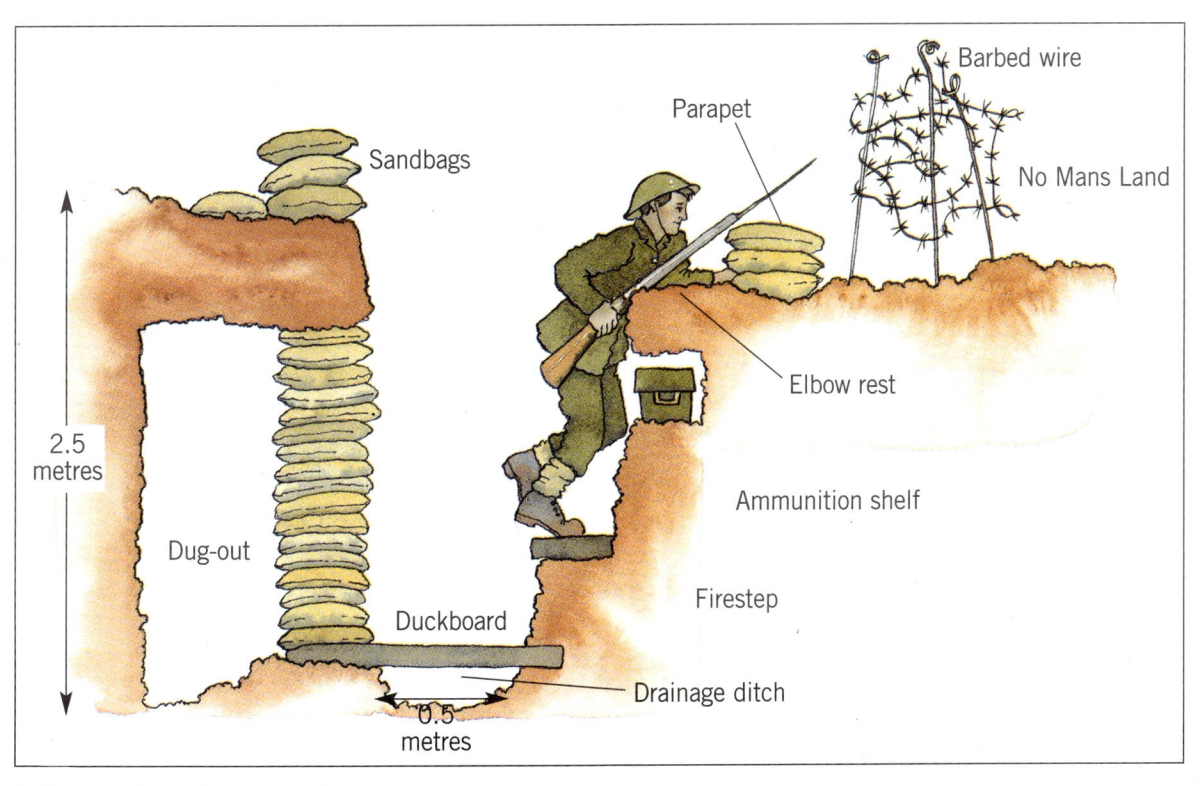

A diagram of trench construction.

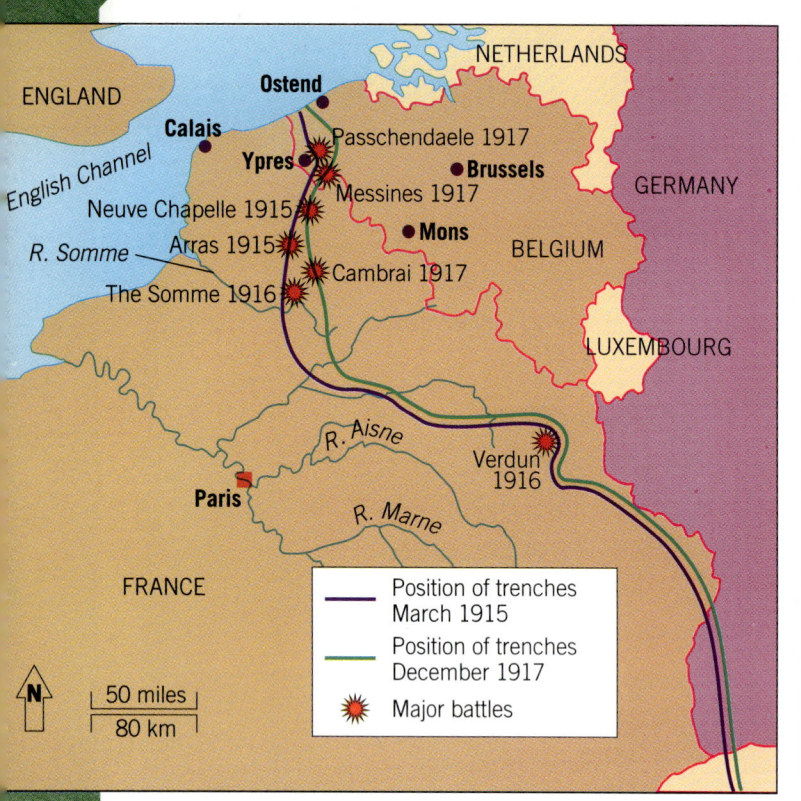

The trench line of the Western Front 1915–17. Notice how little the lines changed in that time.

Source E

Hundreds of dead were strung out like wreckage washed up. They hung there in grotesque postures … It was clear that there were no gaps in the wire at the time of the attack. Concentrated machine gun fire (from the German trenches) had done its work. The Germans must have been reinforcing the wire for months … How did the planners imagine that Tommies (British soldiers) would get through the German wire? Who told them that artillery fire would pound such wire to pieces, making it possible to get through? Any Tommy could have told them that shell fire lifts wire up and drops it down often in a worse tangle than before.

George Coppard wrote this in his diary on 2 July 1916. He was a soldier who survived the first day's fighting at the Battle of the Somme. He was describing the battlefield the day after. On 1 July 20,000 British soldiers were killed and 35,000 injured.

Source D

My dear sweet lassie,

We have been several days in these trenches now and things are very hot indeed – shells, bombs and trench mortars flying about thick and fast.

I was sitting with Charlie (a stretcher bearer) in this dug out when the sharp call came down for 'stretcher bearers!' Charlie darts out like lightning, always alert is he. He returned about two hours later and he was a sight, his hands and clothes covered with blood and his face pale with exhaustion. It appears a shell nearly sent him to glory on his way back — lifted him clean off his feet and dropped him into a dug out.

Frank Cocker's letter to his girlfriend, Evelyn Kershaw, dated 13 July 1915. Frank Cocker arrived in France on 14 April 1915. It was ten days before he saw active service. Between May and June his battalion occasionally relieved troops in the front line. This letter shows his relative inexperience.

Source F

Dusk was falling when from the German trenches rose that strange green cloud of death. In the gathering dark of that awful night they (French soldiers) fought with their terror, running blindly in the gas cloud, and dropping in agony and the slow poison of suffocation covering their dark faces. Hundreds of them fell and died, others lay helpless, froth upon their agonised lips and their racked bodies powerfully sick, with rising nausea at short intervals. They too would die later — a slow lingering death of unimaginable agony.

A British soldier, H Pollard, described the first use of chlorine gas by German troops at the Second Battle of Ypres, 22 April 1915.

Source G

'Gassed.' A painting by J Singer Sargent.

Work it out!

1 What can we learn from these sources about:

   a What happened during the daily life in the trenches

   b What the men felt and thought about trench warfare?

   To help you to answer **a**:
   Make a table of all the sources and list all the information that you can find in each source.

   To help you to answer **b**:
   - Write down for each source the words and phrases that indicate the thoughts of the author about the scene around him. Then explain what point you think he is making.
   - Think about the tone of each source.
   - How does the rhythm of the poems in Sources B and C convey the author's opinions?
   - What is it about Source D that makes it different from the other sources? Why?

2 Sources A, E and F are eye-witness accounts; Sources B and C are poems written by eye-witnesses, and Source D is a letter written home.

   a Which type of source is the most useful in helping us to understand the events of the war in the trenches?

   b Is any one type of source more useful than another in helping us to understand some of the opinions and feelings about the war?

   Explain your answers as fully as you can.

Learning from eye-witnesses

Liberating the concentration camps

The **Allies** had heard news of the mass slaughter of the Jews by the **Nazis** in late 1942, but it was not until mid-1944 that they became aware of the existence of **Auschwitz** and its gas chambers. As the Allied armies liberated central Europe and reached the death camps, the horror of the **Holocaust** was discovered.

The accounts in Sources A–F come from two survivors and one of the liberators. Primo Levi survived Auschwitz and went on to write his autobiography. Gena Turgel was released from Belsen in 1945. Auschwitz was liberated by the Red Army and Belsen by the British.

Source A

The first Russian patrol came in sight of the camp (Auschwitz) about midday on 27 January 1945. Charles and I were the first to see them: we were carrying Somogyi's body to the common grave which was a large open pit. He was the first of our room mates to die. We tipped the stretcher carrying the body on to the stained snow, as the pit was now full, and no other grave was at hand: Charles took off his beret as a salute to both the living and the dead.

An extract from Primo Levi's autobiography.

Source B

The Nazis were walking around for two days still armed, until they were ordered to assemble outside the British headquarters. When they were arrested, I wept with tears.

The Nazis marched past, their faces expressionless and yet still retaining a cocky, arrogant stance. They had been so brainwashed by Hitler into believing that they would win the war that they must have felt a sense of unreality about being arrested.

From Gena Turgel's autobiography describing the liberation of Belsen.

The writers

Primo Levi was an Italian who was captured in 1944 and sent to Auschwitz. He wrote his autobiography after the war and it was published in two parts, the first part, *If This is a Man* was published in 1958, and the second, *The Truce, A Survivor's Journey Home from Auschwitz* in 1968.

Gena Turgel was born in Cracow, Poland in 1923. After the invasion by the Nazis in September 1939, she was confined to a ghetto and spent three years in concentration camps or extermination camps: she was held at Plazov, Auschwitz and Belsen. She married **Norman Turgel**, one of the liberators of Belsen, and lives outside London. Her autobiography, *I Light a Candle* was published in 1987, and contains the recollections of her husband, as well as her own.

Source C

When the gates opened and the tanks entered the camp, we heard voices speaking in all languages through the loudspeakers: English, Polish, German. 'We have come to liberate you. You are all free. The Nazis have nothing to say to you'. It was the happiest moment of my life, and one of the most fantastic experiences that could happen to anyone.

The British troops came to the door of the hospital (where I was working). The Nazis were still there, with pistols in their holsters, and we were still afraid. It was a strange combination and we couldn't understand it: here on one side, the British; there, on the other side, armed Nazi guards.

From the autobiography *I Light a Candle* by Gena Turgel.

Source D

I was a sergeant in the 53 Field Security section of the British Intelligence Corps. We had instructions to take over Belsen camp, and on Sunday 15 April 1945, at 3 pm one of our tanks entered the camp, and we followed on foot. The scenes which greeted us were like something out of a horror film. People everywhere were dying. In some cases they were so far gone that you couldn't tell whether they were young or old, woman or man.

To survive, they had been reduced to cannibalism. Some of the bodies I saw had parts of the flesh missing. As a young soldier who had witnessed the killing of soldiers and animals on many occasions, I found this a shocking experience. I had seen my share of battle casualties, but to see thousands of innocent people in a camp being starved to death, murdered, poisoned, was beyond belief.

Norman Turgel's account of the liberation of Belsen concentration camp.

Source E

Thousands of pairs of shoes belonging to victims who had been murdered were found in the death camps.

SOURCE F

The first person I arrested was Josef Kramer, the Camp Commandant, known as the 'Beast of Belson'.

When I arrested him I said in German: 'I'm a Jew'. He said: 'That's impossible. There are no Jews in the army. We are killing them all'. I said: 'There are thousands of them in the British Army'. But he was still adamant.

I was very proud of being a Jew who had arrested one of the most notorious gangsters in Nazi Germany.

There were lampshades which he (Kramer) had had made in Auschwitz from human skin, and in the kitchens we found bags of ground glass which was used to doctor the inmates' soup.

Norman Turgel describes his experiences as one of the liberators of Belsen.

Work it out!

What would you suggest should be done to try to discover more evidence about the extent of the Holocaust – the numbers of dead, the history of the camps, the purpose behind them?

You have been with the liberating forces and have been asked to explain to Allied Headquarters what has been discovered at Auschwitz and Belsen.

Make notes for your talk, based round the following points:

- Describe what you saw on entering the camp
- Explain what the survivors have told you
- Give any other information you have about the liberation of other camps: how similar were the conditions?
- Explain what you think should be done for the survivors
- Suggest what you think should happen to the Nazis responsible for the camps.

CONTROVERSIAL HISTORIAN LOSES LIBEL CASE

BACKGROUND

David Irving is a well-known historian who has controversial views on the Holocaust. For example, in 1999 he told a large audience in the German town of Dresden that: 'The Holocaust of Jews in the gas chambers of Auschwitz is an invention'. He also said that the stories of gas chambers were just propaganda used by the Allies in the war.

WHY WAS THERE A LIBEL CASE?

Penguin has published a book by the American author Deborah Lipstadt saying that Irving twisted history to make Hitler look better. Lipstadt accused Irving of doing this because he is anti-Jewish and pro-Nazi. Irving objected to this view and sued Lipstadt and Penguin.

WHAT HAPPENED?

Despite passionate speeches by Irving, the judge did not agree that what Lipstadt had written was wrong. The judge said, 'I am satisfied that in most instances cited by the defendants, Irving has misrepresented what the evidence reveals'. In other words, Irving's controversial views on the Holocaust were more propaganda than fact.

Despite overwhelming evidence, some people have tried to argue that the gas chambers were not used for mass killing. One of these is David Irving. In early 2000 he took a publisher, Penguin, and an author to court for accusing him of allowing his anti-Jewish views to cloud his historical judgement. Irving lost the case and had to pay large sums towards Penguin's costs.

Assessing the evidence

Was the bombing of Hiroshima and Nagasaki justified?

The state of the war in 1945

Germany, Japan's ally, had surrendered in May, and the Italian leader Mussolini had been executed. Japan was fighting alone. American planes had control of the skies over Japan, and in March 1945, 80,000 Japanese had died from fire bombs dropped on Tokyo. This was more than were killed in England during the whole of the Blitz. The Americans captured the islands of Iwo Jima and Okinawa with terrible casulties on both sides. The people of Japan were starving, but the Japanese government refused to consider negotiation.

Dropping the bombs

On 6 August 1945 an American bomber plane called the *Enola Gay* dropped the world's first atomic bomb on the Japanese city of Hiroshima. The bomb killed about 80,000 people immediately. The Japanese did not surrender. Two days later the USSR invaded Manchuria, in keeping with the Allies' agreement at Potsdam. Three days later a second bomb was dropped on the city of Nagasaki and about 40,000 people died. Many more died afterwards from radiation sickness. On 14 August the Japanese surrendered to the Allies.

The Kamikaze pilots

The Japanese were so determined not to give in that they were literally prepared to commit suicide. Kamikaze or suicide pilots would volunteer for missions in which they became 'living bombs'. The pilot would take off in an obsolete plane, packed with explosives, then fly directly at an enemy warship. When the US forces attacked Okinawa, some 2000 Kamikaze pilots died, sinking 30 US warships.

Source A

Bear in mind the fact that to be captured is a disgrace to the army. Also your parents and family will never be able to hold up their heads again. Always save the last bullet for yourself.

An extract from the Japanese army manual issued during the war.

How to win the war?

The Allies had demanded 'unconditional surrender', but this was seen by the Japanese as a threat to their imperial system, and they fought on. Following Germany's surrender in 1945 the Allies broadcast to the Japanese that 'unconditional surrender' did not necessarily mean the deposition of the emperor. The Allies issued an ultimatum to the Japanese on 26 July, threatening 'the utter destruction of the homeland'. This they again ignored. Instead, they were trying to persuade the Russians to act as mediators.

President Truman knew that dropping the bomb might be called a crime against humanity. He also knew that the Japanese had not surrendered despite huge casualties after conventional bombing by the US airforce. The Japanese were ferocious fighters and they were prepared to commit suicide or starve rather than surrender. This meant that to defeat them the Americans would lose huge numbers of men.

Source B

We have to hope for the possibility of preventing an Okinawa from one end of Japan to the other.

Said by President Truman when considering the future plan of attacks on Japan in the spring of 1945.

Source C

The dropping of the two bombs stopped the war and saved millions of lives. It was just the same as getting a bigger gun than the other side had to win the war and that's what it was used for.

President Truman, speaking at Columbia University, USA in 1959.

The Battle of Okinawa April–June 1945

US casualties – over 35 per cent of the fighting force.

Over 5000 sailors – more than at Pearl Harbor
Over 9000 soldiers, airmen and marines

Japanese casualties

Population of Okinawa – between 70,000 and 160,000

Taken prisoner – 7400

Fighting force – 110,000 killed or committed suicide, refusing to surrender.

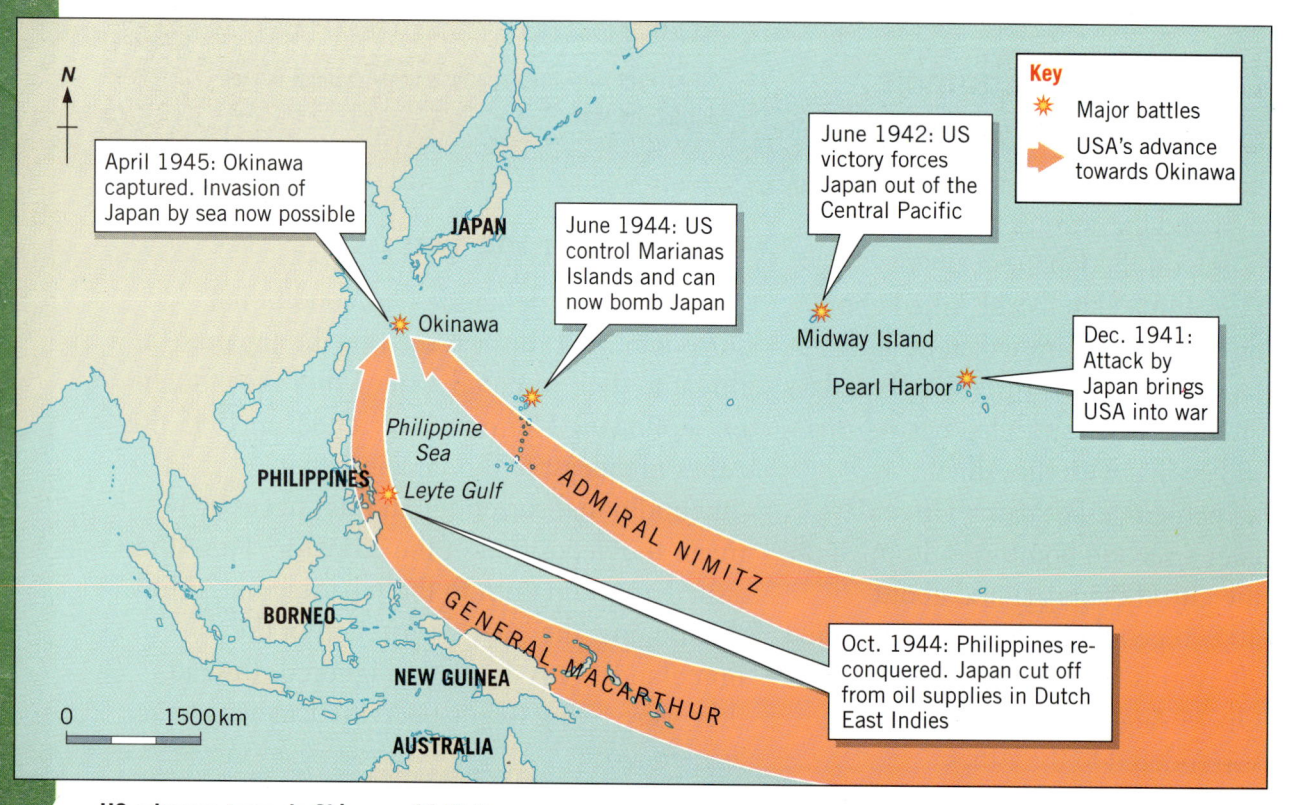

US advance towards Okinawa, 1942-5.

- April 1945: Okinawa captured. Invasion of Japan by sea now possible
- June 1944: US control Marianas Islands and can now bomb Japan
- June 1942: US victory forces Japan out of the Central Pacific
- Dec. 1941: Attack by Japan brings USA into war
- Oct. 1944: Philippines re-conquered. Japan cut off from oil supplies in Dutch East Indies

Key: Major battles, USA's advance towards Okinawa

SOURCE D

A photograph of Hiroshima after the bomb.

Reasons for and against

Since 1940 scientists in the USA had been working on a new bomb that could destroy whole cities.

- It was argued that a great deal of money had been spent on developing the bomb and the expense could only be justified by using it. Thousands of innocent civilians, including women and children would die, but had not thousands already died from the use of conventional bombs?

- Others have argued that the US commanders wanted to use the new bomb in order to show the Soviet Union how powerful the USA was. This was because the American Chiefs of Staff were concerned about the power of the Soviet forces in Manchuria, and the Japanese attempts to use the Russians as mediators.

- However, many said that Japan was close to starvation and defeat, and would have surrendered soon in any case.

After the drop

SOURCE E

Mountain of smoke

Captain Parsons, who went in the 'plane to observe the effects of the bomb, said: 'The whole thing was tremendous and awe-inspiring. After the missile had been released I sighed and stood back for the shock. When it came the men aboard with me gasped "My God," and what had been Hiroshima was a mountain of smoke like a giant mushroom'.

'A thousand feet above the ground was a great mass of dust, boiling, swirling and extending over most of the city. Soon afterwards small fires sprang up on the edge of the town, but the town itself was entirely obscured. We stayed around for two or three minutes and by that time the smoke had risen to 40,000 ft (13,300 m.). As we watched the top cone of white smoke broke off, but another soon formed.'

A report from the British newspaper *The Manchester Guardian* 9 August 1945.

SOURCE F

As we staggered along, we were joined by many who had escaped death for the moment. Many were soldiers who had been out working and had looked up at the blinding flash. They became victims of direct burns. The upper half of their bodies and faces were burned consistently, leaving just the tips of their heads where their caps had protected them. Their skin was charcoal black and hung loosely from their bodies, and body fluid and body oil oozed out.

An extract from *Hiroshima, An Eyewitness Account* by June Weden, 1945.

SOURCE G

Survivors began to notice in themselves a strange form of illness. It consisted of vomiting, loss of appetite, diarrhoea with large amounts of blood, purple spots on the skin, bleeding from the mouth, loss of hair and usually death.

A Japanese eye-witness account of radiation sickness.

SOURCE H

It is my opinion that the use of this barbarous weapon was of no material help in our war against Japan. The Japanese were already defeated and were ready to surrender because of the effective sea blockade and the successful use of conventional bombing. The scientists and others wanted to make this test because of the vast sums that had been spent on the project.

Comment by Admiral William D Leahy, Chief of Staff to the US President, 1945.

Work it out!

Read carefully all the information given about why the atomic bombs were dropped. Then look at the effects of using the bombs and the reasons against using atomic weapons.

President Truman of the United States of America has asked you to write his speech for him in 100 words, giving the reasons for dropping an atomic bomb over Hiroshima and then another over Nagasaki.

Understanding short-term causes

The development of a multi-cultural society

Britain faced many problems after the end of the Second World War. The government had promised to introduce a '**welfare state**' in which nobody would suffer poverty as a result of unemployment and there was to be a free National Health Service. These plans would be very expensive. Britain had huge war debts to the USA and cities had to be rebuilt following the Blitz. Civilians and service men and women had lost their lives and there was an acute shortage of workers. The government decided to encourage workers from the empire to **emigrate** to Britain.

The *Windrush* arrives

In June 1948, the SS *Empire Windrush* docked in Britain. It carried 492 job seekers from Jamaica, many of whom had served in the forces helping the Allied war effort.

They were given a warm welcome in the press. Other ships followed, but in 1951 the census figures show that there were only about 15,000 **immigrants** born in the West Indies living in Britain. The years between 1955 and 1962 saw the bulk of the arrivals.

This was partly because in 1952 the USA brought in controls to limit the numbers of migrants who could enter the USA from the Caribbean. Britain was now the only industrial country where they could go to find work. The numbers entering Britain each year during the 50s closely reflected the number of jobs available. The news of a labour shortage in Britain would instantly encourage more migrants, whereas a shortage of jobs in Britain would delay departures from the Caribbean.

Source A

SS Empire Windrush arriving in Britain in 1948.

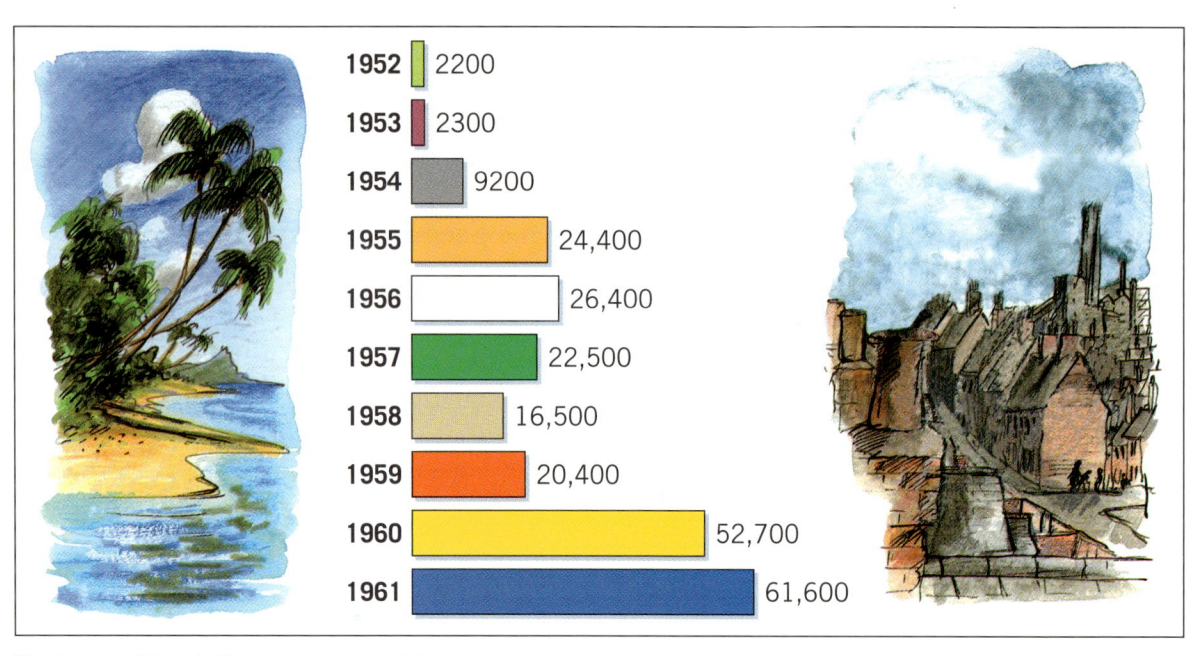

Year	Number
1952	2200
1953	2300
1954	9200
1955	24,400
1956	26,400
1957	22,500
1958	16,500
1959	20,400
1960	52,700
1961	61,600

Numbers of West Indian emigrants to Britain.

What did they find?

The West Indian people who arrived in England felt the cold, saw chimneys for the first time and met with frequent examples of indifference and discrimination. Many were Anglicans (belonged to the Church of England), but were asked not to attend Church services as their presence upset the congregation. Many employers would only take a black person if they could not find a white one. Many landlords refused to have black people as their tenants.

Source B

And what has made them leave Jamaica? In most cases, lack of work. They spoke independently, but unanimously (as one), of a blight that has come upon the West Indies since those who served America and Britain during the war returned home. The cost of living is high, wages are low. Many can earn no wages. Some had been unemployed for two years. One of them considered his chances in Britain (he was a builder), and said laconically, 'If I survive – so good; if I don't survive – so good.'

From a newspaper article describing the arrival of the SS Empire Windrush.

Source C

Donald Hinds arrived on the SS *Auriga* in 1955. He quickly found a job with London Transport. He became the fifth black bus conductor at Brixton bus garage. It was difficult to get a place to live; many people refused to let rooms to black people, and the rents were immediately higher.

From Donald Hinds' autobiography. Donald went on to take school exams and a university degree and trained as a teacher.

Source D

When our parents arrived after the Second World War, they knew themselves to be British citizens – many of them had fought as such in uniform during the war. But in Britain it was as if they had never existed. They met an attitude of racial superiority. If their citizenship was to mean more than the paper on which it was written, it would be necessary for the whole country to reassess...what it meant to be British.

Extract from *Windrush, The Irresistible Rise of Multi-Racial Britain* written by Mike Phillips and Trevor Phillips, published in 1998.

Source E

Gradually the friendly, if patronising interest shown by the newspapers in 1948 changed. The immigrants were seen as a threat, as scapegoats for every problem of crime and poor housing. There was a grumbling attitude that black people should not have been in the country at all, illustrated by the phrase 'Why don't you go back where you came from?'

Adapted from *Windrush, The Irresistible Rise of Multi-Racial Britain* by Mike Phillips and Trevor Phillips, published in 1998.

Source F

Well, I went to England in the fifties – 1954 – and of course, I was looking for a better life. I was a young man, and I wanted to see what the outside world was like, and it was a good thing that I did go to England. You name it, I've done it, in England, and I enjoy it.

From an interview with Jo Whitter, who came from Jamaica and went on to be a successful property developer.

Even if many of the first migrants had intended to return to their homeland, many ended up staying in Britain. They stayed for the work and for the money they could earn, and also because they had come to improve their lot in life, and would not go back until this was achieved. As time went on, communities became more settled. The aggressive attitude of some white people only served to increase the West Indians' sense of purpose.

In 1961 the Commonwealth Immigration Act limited the numbers of migrants to Britain. There had been growing concern about the numbers of people arriving with little or no money and no jobs to go to.

Riots in 1958 in Nottingham and Notting Hill Gate, London, hastened the government's decision to bring in immigration controls and news of the act sparked off a rush of immigrants to Britain before the law took effect. Many men who had come over in the 1950s sent for their wives and families to join them. And people continued to come to find work, to benefit from the British education system and because they thought there would be a better future in Britain.

Source G

A young black woman bus conductress in 1962.

Work it out!

1. What did Britain stand to gain from West Indian immigration?
2. What did West Indians stand to gain by emigrating to Britain? Use all the information provided for you.

Massacre at Amritsar

From 1900 onwards, more and more countries that were part of the **British Empire** were demanding freedom to rule themselves. In India there were **nationalist** demonstrations, strikes and even violence against the British. The British did not want to lose India, which brought a lot of wealth to Britain. The situation became more and more tense. However, when the First World War (1914–18) broke out, the Indian people were loyal to the British. They sent soldiers to fight against Germany. They helped to run businesses and the government, as British administrators went to war. The British gratefully promised reform. But when the war ended they made no reforms. In 1919 British laws called the 'black acts' restricted Indian rights even more, including the right to hold public meetings. It also gave the British the right to imprison **extremists** for up to two years without trial. Various nationalist leaders urged people to oppose the 'black acts'. There was rioting all over India.

Peaceful protest?

Most Indians wanted freedom from British rule, but they did not agree about how to win it. Some believed the British would never willingly give up power – their actions after the war proved this – so they should be forced out. Other groups thought that violence against the British would be bad for India. They wanted to use peaceful action to disrupt British businesses. M K Gandhi, a young lawyer, organised the first of the 'peaceful' **general strikes** to start just five days after the 'black acts' were passed.

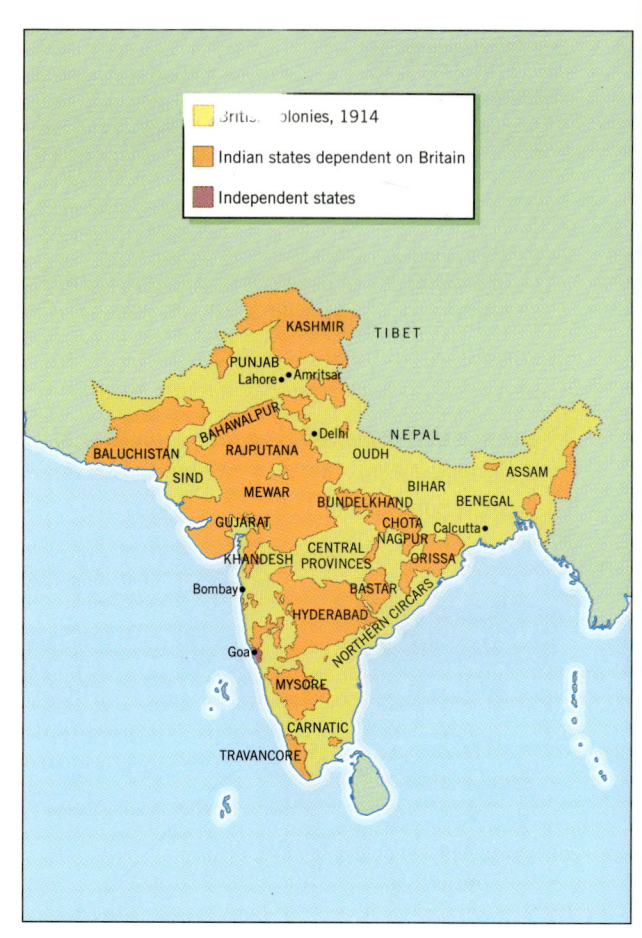

India in 1914.

Violent action

The problem was that any protest, even one that was intended to be peaceful, could erupt into violence. On the first day of the strikes organised by Gandhi there was fighting in Delhi between strikers and those who refused to strike. The violence spread and the police were called in, then the army. The soldiers opened fire on the protesters and eight of the strikers were killed. Up and down the country there was violence that ended with British troops firing on unarmed civilians and killing them. Troops were quicker to react violently when confronted with an angry crowd. This gained the nationalists more support, especially in the Punjab. It also made the British more edgy about the possibility of a violent uprising aimed at driving them out of India.

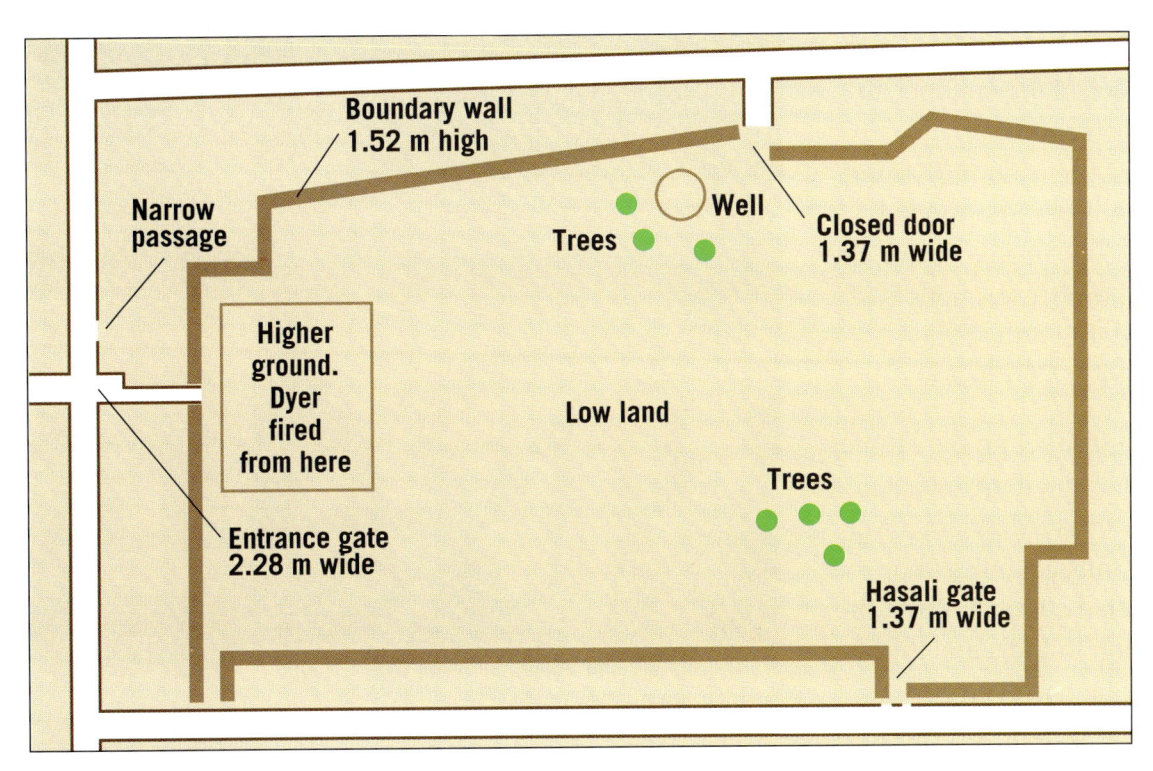

The Jallianwala Bagh.

Diagram labels:
- Boundary wall 1.52 m high
- Narrow passage
- Trees
- Well
- Closed door 1.37 m wide
- Higher ground. Dyer fired from here
- Low land
- Trees
- Entrance gate 2.28 m wide
- Hasali gate 1.37 m wide

Riots in Amritsar

In the Punjabi city of Amritsar, on 10 April 1919, demonstrators marched on the British **compound** to protest about the arrest of local nationalist leaders. British troops fired on them and killed several, starting a riot. Two British banks were looted and their managers hacked to death. The town hall, telegraph office and railway depot were set alight. In all, five Europeans were killed (including a female **missionary**, who also worked as a doctor). Several more were wounded. General Reginald Dyer was sent to restore order and stop more disturbances. He gave orders that there should be no meetings. He also introduced a 'crawling order'. Indians who wished to go up the street where the English missionary had been killed had to do so on their hands and knees, in penance for her death. While he later argued that this had only been enforced once, the fact that he passed such an order seemed to many people to sum up all that was wrong with British rule in India.

Amritsar had a large walled area, the Jallianwalla Bagh, that was used for markets, religious festivals and meetings. On 13 April people from nearby villages came there for a Hindu festival. A group of protesters met there, too. There are estimates of the number of people that were there, ranging from 10,000 to 20,000 unarmed men, women and children.

Work it out!

1. Why might the people of India have felt betrayed by the British when the First World War ended?

2. Write outline speeches for a nationalist debate over whether to use violence or peaceful methods to gain independence from British rule. Remember you are writing from an Indian point of view. Think about:
   - what the British have promised
   - what the British actually did
   - how likely it is they will give power away
   - the problems violence will cause.

Dyer had under 100 troops. He blocked the entrance to the Bagh and his troops opened fire without warning. They killed and wounded about 2000 people (again, the exact number was hotly argued over – the British estimate was far lower).

The British set up the Hunter Commission to investigate the Amritsar Massacre. Dyer was dismissed, but said he had acted correctly, given the situation in India and the orders he had been given. Some British people saw him as a hero. Why did he massacre these innocent civilians?

Source A

A still from the film Gandhi showing Dyer's troops opening fire on the crowds.

Source B

Question: You did not warn the gathering to disperse before you opened fire. Did you think your small force might be attacked?

Dyer: No, I issued no warning. The situation was very serious. It was no longer a question of simply dispersing the crowd. I had to produce a sufficient impression of strength not only on those that were there, but throughout the Punjab.

Question: When did you first decide to fire?

Dyer: When I first heard of the meeting.

From evidence given by General Dyer to the Hunter Commission.

Source C

I shot to preserve India for the Empire and to protect English people who looked to me for protection. And now I am dismissed for doing my duty — my horrible, dirty duty. I had to shoot. I had thirty seconds to make up my mind about what action to take. What would have happened if I had not shot? I and my little force would have been swept away and then what would have happened?

From an interview given by General Dyer after he had been dismissed following the Hunter Commission.

Source D

General Dyer received an urgent request for help from Amritsar, where disturbances had been very serious — including the murder of bank managers and a brutal attack on an English woman doctor, left for dead. On his arrival, he found the local police could not cope with the situation. He issued orders against violence and damage to property and against meetings of more than four people. Despite this the Indians gathered in large numbers at Jallianwalla Bagh — estimates vary between 5000 and 30,000. It was then that Dyer, who was in command of a little force of 25 British riflemen, 25 Indian riflemen, 40 Ghurkhas armed with knives and two armoured cars, gave the order to fire.

Part of a report in the British newspaper *The Daily Mail*, 4 May 1920.

SOURCE E

The previous episodes at Amritsar, the rioting and murders, are well known, as are the circumstances under which General Dyer, with a very small force, opened fire on a dense crowd in a confined space. They fired 1650 times, killing 379 persons, and possibly wounding three times as many. The government has since said that, while there were problems in the Punjab, Dyer was not entitled to make an example of an unarmed crowd that had committed no act of violence, had made no attempts to oppose him by force. Many of them must have been unaware that they were breaking his order not to hold meetings.

Part of a report in the British newspaper *The Times*, 27 May 1920.

Divided reactions

When we consider the way people reacted to the massacre at Amritsar, we have to remember that news did not spread as quickly or as widely as it does now. News of the massacre was slow to leak out, and reports about what exactly happened varied. Reactions were mixed. Most people were horrified by what General Dyer did. Many people, including Gandhi, who had previously wanted a peaceful move to independence, now saw co-operation with the British as impossible. A few saw Dyer as a hero – acting to prevent terrible violence spilling over and sweeping the country. Dyer was dismissed. His actions were condemned in the House of Commons. Yet the House of Lords praised his actions and his sacking led to the formation of the Dyer Appreciation Fund, which collected enough money to present Dyer with a gilt-covered 'sword of honour' and a 'purse' of money. This collection was advertised in both British and Indian papers. Both British and Indian families contributed to the fund.

After Amritsar

Directly after the massacre, Dyer was still in charge in Amritsar. He was still fearful of a rising. He therefore imposed martial law, meaning that the army, not the police or local government officials, were now in charge. He maintained the ban on meetings. He also kept his troops patrolling Amritsar, stopping 'suspicious' people — which seemed to apply to any Indian male they felt like harassing. He even left the 'crawling order' in force. Once the Hunter Commission was set up martial law was abandoned and, after Dyer's dismissal, things calmed down again. But violence was still simmering. In 1947 there was another outbreak of rioting up and down India, which led to independence being granted finally in August 1948. One of the places where the rioting was fiercest was Amritsar.

Work it out!

1. How many Indian people were there at the Jallianwalla Bagh on 13 April 1919 and why were they there?

2. In Source B Dyer gives his evidence to the Commission that later decided to dismiss him. Source C is part of his statement to a newspaper after his dismissal. Does this mean that the reasons he gives in Source C for opening fire are more accurate? Explain your answer.

3. Do the two newspaper reports, Sources D and E (written after the Commission published its findings) feel the same about Dyer's actions?

4. a What sorts of Indian and British people might have supported Dyer's actions?
   b What sorts of Indian and British people might have condemned Dyer's actions?

5. Why do you think Dyer acted as he did? Explain your answer.

Chinese women – bound to the home?

Well into the twentieth century people in China still practised footbinding on the feet of young girls. Footbinding is where the feet of girls, from the age of about six, are kept permanently wrapped in tight bandages. The bandages squeeze the foot in on itself, bending (sometimes breaking) the bones. Binding makes feet much smaller. By the time the girls became women, their feet were permanently **distorted**.

Chinese views on bound feet

In China, small feet were seen as beautiful. In a society where marriage was still the main aim of women, girls were told that they would be more likely to get a husband if they had 'beautiful' feet. Bound feet were also a sign of **status**. Women with bound feet could not walk far, or work in factories or fields. They did not work and were waited on by other people, so they were, obviously, important.

Effects of footbinding

Footbinding had the effect of forcing women to spend most of their time indoors, in their homes or visiting women in similar circumstances. They were dependent on their husbands and some husbands treated their wives very badly. Chinese society, like many others at the time, accepted that women might be badly treated, but expected that they would stay put and put up with it. However, the fact that they were, quite literally, unable to run away because of their bound feet was yet another obstacle for any woman whose husband harmed her.

SOURCE A

A Chinese woman's feet deformed by lifelong binding.

SOURCE B

In her tiny embroidered shoes, her clothing hiding her swollen and deformed ankles, the Chinese girl took tiny exaggerated steps, leaning on the arm of one of her servants. The way her body swayed as she tottered on her crippled feet was the famous 'lily walk'. Chinese writers all through the ages praised this walk, even though, when her bandages were renewed, the stench of crushed flesh was appalling.

An English writer described in 1972 the effect of footbinding.

SOURCE C

When we are still young girls our mothers take out snow-white bandages and bind them round our feet. Even when we go to bed at night, we are not allowed to loosen them in the least bit. The result is that the flesh peels away and the bones bend and buckle under. The only reason for doing all this is to make sure that our friends and neighbours will all say: 'Haven't the girls in that family all got lovely small feet!'

Qiu Jin, a Chinese woman, wrote about the practice of footbinding in 1906.

SOURCE D

Mei Ling's ankles are deformed, her feet are half bound. When she was a little girl her feet had been bound by her mother. Then came the revolution and the anti-footbinding movement. All women under the age of 30 were urged to unbind their feet. Revolutionaries went from place to place urging women to unbind their feet and cut their long hair. When some women refused the revolutionaries cut their hair and unbound their feet by force. Mei Ling unbound her own feet, although this caused her as much pain as the original binding had done. She was too old for her feet to regain their natural shape, so she wears her feet half bound.

Written by Agnes Smedley, who lived in China in the 1930s.

Work it out!

1. How does the writer in Source B feel about footbinding? Explain how you came to your decision.
2. The writer in Source C seems to disapprove of footbinding. What evidence is there in the source that the mothers who bound their girls' feet were not doing it out of cruelty?
3. You are going to produce a pamphlet showing EITHER that footbinding should be stopped OR that it should not be stopped. Decide which.
   a. Which source would you use in this pamphlet? Why?
   b. Produce a poster to go with such a pamphlet.

Exploding rats – the gadgets of the SOE

In July 1940, less than a year after the start of the Second World War, the British Government set up the Special Operations Executive (SOE). The **Nazis** were taking over more and more of Europe and 'occupying' it. Local people set up groups to work secretly against the Germans. These were called 'resistance' groups. The job of the SOE was to help organise resistance to the German occupation all across Europe. Winston Churchill said it was to 'set Europe ablaze'. The work of resistance groups in Europe, and the heroic deaths of many of the resistance fighters, is well known. So are the SOE plans to feed the Germans false information about **Allied** plans. Less well known, until recently, were the gadgets invented for SOE agents.

Scientists at Aston House, in Stevenage, invented ways of carrying secret codes written on thin silk and hidden in clothing. Radios were made as small as possible to fit a variety of hiding places (including bundles of firewood). Folding canoes and one-man submarines were designed to help agents move about secretly. Many of the inventions tried to make daily life as dangerous and unpredictable as possible for the enemy. So explosives were concealed in everyday objects, from milk bottles to cigarette packets. These would cause small, constant disruptions as well as the more obvious blowing up of railway lines or bridges to disrupt communications.

Exploding coal and dung

The SOE made about 140 different shapes of exploding coal. Their handbook for secret agents explained how it was done: *A hollow cast is made of a piece of coal, in two sections. The centre is filled with plastic explosive and the two halves are fixed together. The coal is finished off by painting it with black shellac (an enamel paint) and coal dust.* The SOE wanted to supply enemy train stations with this coal. At this time, trains were still steam trains, fuelled by coal. If the exploding coal was fed into a train's furnace, it could damage the engine so badly that it could no longer be used or, as the handbook put it, *at least make the profession of locomotive driver highly unpopular.*

The SOE followed the same system to make exploding dung. Dung from horses, cows, camels, elephants and mules was collected from London Zoo. The realistic casts were to be sent all over the world. The horse manure was for Europe. The camel dung was to be sent to North Africa. The mule, cow and elephant dung was intended for the Far East. In every case the dung was to be put on the roads in the hope that the enemy would tread on it or drive over it to set it off.

Irritating the enemy

Not all of the SOE's plans for disrupting the enemy's daily life used explosives. Some were far simpler. Agents were told about the effectiveness of **itching powder** (best applied to the inside of underclothes) against the enemy. The local resistance workers were to persuade the washer women, who cleaned clothes for the Germans, into using the powder. This was certainly done at least once. The SOE agents in Troyes, France, got the underwear of a German submarine crew treated with itching powder. Did it work? There were rumours that the crew surrendered because they all became ill with a skin disease. Whether the rumour was true or just put about by the SOE to raise morale is another matter!

Primer

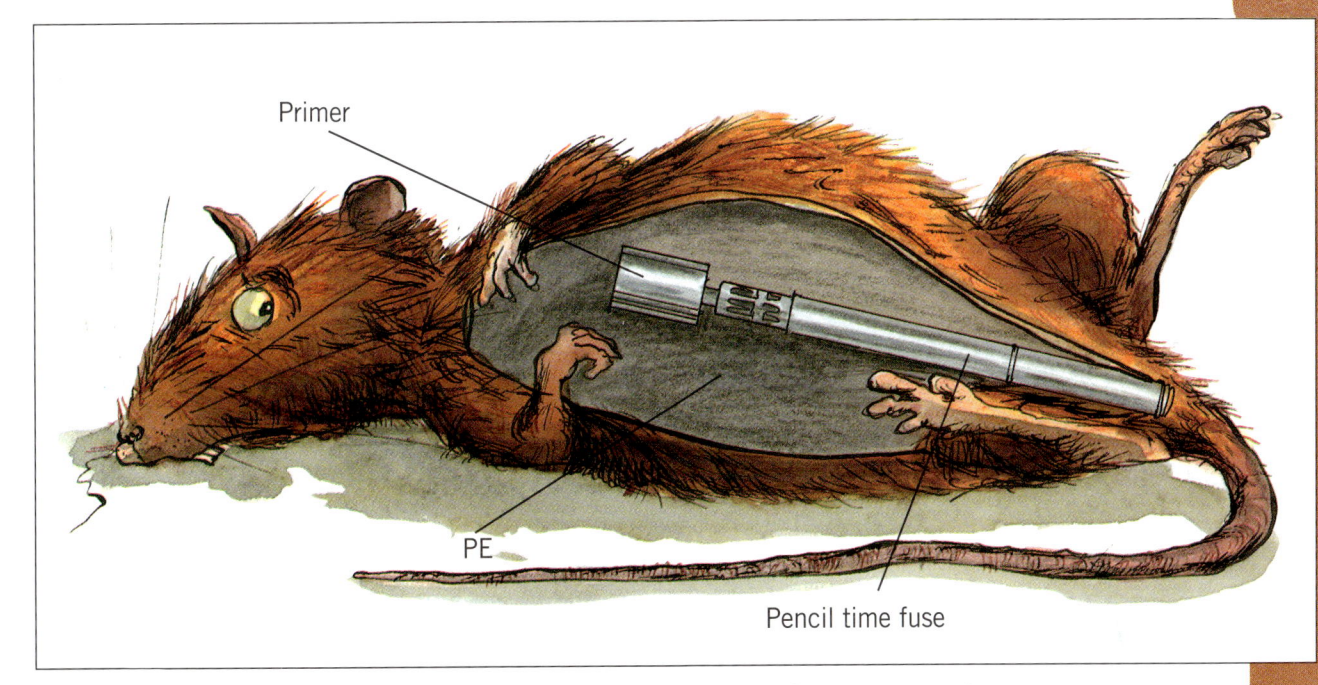

PE

Pencil time fuse

A modern artist's humorous version of the SOE design to show how exploding rats were made.

The case of the exploding rats

One SOE scheme involved exploding rats. An agent in Britain pretended to be a student who needed rats for laboratory experiments. He collected up a great many of them. The rats were killed and skinned. The skins were then filled with **plastic explosive** (**PE**) and a **fuse**. The idea was to take the rats across to Europe. Resistance agents would then put the rats in with the coal near a boiler. The person stoking the boiler would throw the rat on too, causing a huge explosion. The first container of dead rats was made ready and sent over to France. SOE agents there were horrified when the Germans got hold of the container before the rats could be taken out and used. The Germans examined the container, found the rats and worked out what they were to be used for.

While the SOE knew that this was the first container that had been sent to Europe, the Germans did not. The Germans began to worry that there were already hundreds of exploding rats lurking all over France and the rest of occupied Europe. They took the rats round to all their training centres and organised lectures to alert troops to the danger the rats presented. They even organised hunts for them. All this wasted their time and shifted their attention away from other resistance activity. So, despite the fact that they were never used, the exploding rats caused a great deal of disruption and were, an official report admitted, '*a much greater success to us than if the rats had actually been used.*'

Work it out!

'The SOE department that organised all this itching powder and exploding rats stuff was just childish and a huge waste of time and money. The people who invented these things and made them up could have been used in much more sensible war work.'

Do you agree with this statement? Explain your answer.

'Got any gum, chum?' – US troops in Britain

The USA joined the Second World War on 11 December 1941. All through 1942, US forces arrived in Britain in ever-increasing numbers. The USA was too far away for its troops or planes to go straight to Europe. Britain became the departure point for US troops bound for Europe and the US airforce also set up bases in Britain. The US troops were called GIs, after their uniforms, said to be marked 'Government Issue'. The British and US governments stressed the need for unity. The US army produced a guidebook called *A Short Guide to Great Britain* to help their soldiers to fit in. Meanwhile, the British produced a leaflet called *Meet the Americans*.

While governments stressed unity, it was the differences that caught everyone's eye. One small boy, watching US troops arrive in Aylesbury, turned to his mother and asked, 'Are they real, Mummy?'. US troops were seen as loud, overconfident and, in what soon became a catch-phrase among British troops, 'overpaid, oversexed and over here'. Certainly there were British soldiers who came home, either after the war or on **leave**, to find that their wives or girlfriends were expecting the babies of GIs. However, whether there were as many of these cases as people came to believe is uncertain. Some of these stories were told about 'a friend of a friend'. But they confirmed prejudices about GIs. Why were the Americans seen in this way and is it a fair representation of them?

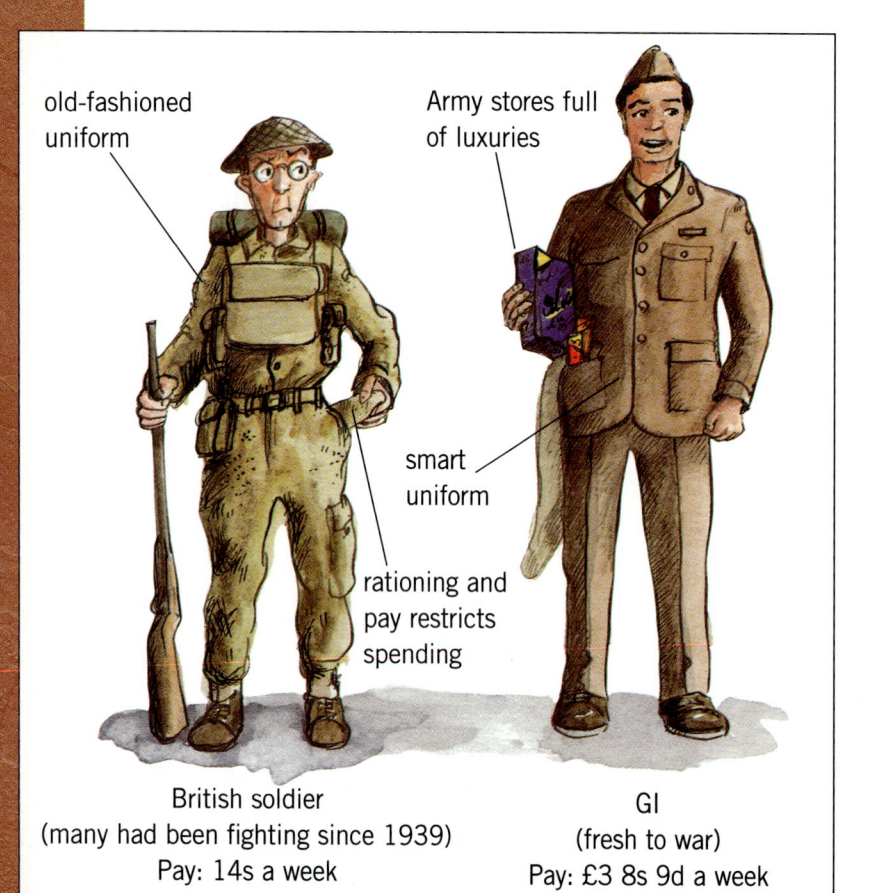

British soldier
(many had been fighting since 1939)
Pay: 14s a week

- old-fashioned uniform
- Army stores full of luxuries
- smart uniform
- rationing and pay restricts spending

GI
(fresh to war)
Pay: £3 8s 9d a week

The US view

The most evident truth of all is that in their major ways of life, the British and American people are much alike. They speak the same language. They both believe in an elected government, in freedom of worship, in freedom of speech.

The British view

And because we have unity under the skin, we men of the shires [the various counties of England] march together, endure together and win together. It is in exactly the same spirit that we shall learn to march with the Americans. We must be willing to like each other – willing because our common cause demands it.

Source A

GIs give out presents at a Christmas party.

Source B

Crossing the ocean doesn't automatically make you a hero. There are housewives in aprons and youngsters in knee pants [shorts] who have lived through more bombing through air raids than many of our soldiers faced during the last war…
If you are standing in line, you will be queuing, pronounced cueing…
'Bum' has a very different meaning in Britain …

Some extracts from *A Short Guide to Great Britain* produced by the US Army.

Source C

It had snowed heavily, so we went sledging. A US army lorry came by and some GIs got out to watch. One asked for a go on my sledge. I let him. It was funny, because he fell off halfway down. After the GIs had stopped laughing they piled back into the lorry and left. About an hour later they were back with a sledge – a wooden bench bolted to a sheet of corrugated iron. We were very impressed – especially when eight of them got on it. They spent the afternoon racing and larking about with us. I think that's what we like best about them, their sense of fun.

Allen Coyne, evacuated during the war, met GIs from a US army base close by.

Source D

They were so gorgeous. They had beautiful uniforms; they all looked like film stars. And those accents! They were so sexy.

They could get anything from the stores on their bases. Things we hadn't seen in ages – chocolate, cigarettes, stockings. Mind you, some of them expected sex in return.

Some wanted a 'cute British' wife to take home. Lots of the girls wanted to go, too. Who wouldn't, when they treated you so nicely, like a princess, and were promising to take you back to a movieland country that was bigger, richer and full of opportunities.

Comments by various women about the GIs they met during the war.

Work it out!

1. a. How does the US army pamphlet illustrate differences in language and attitudes between US and British troops?
   b. What other differences were there? Give examples from several sources.
   c. Why did both governments try to ignore these differences?
2. Why do you think the GIs might be more full of fun, as the boy in Source C says?
3. Which source would you use to show that the GIs were a good thing, not 'oversexed, overpaid and over here'?

A difference of opinion?

One of the most noticeable differences between the British and Americans was their view on what the British called 'the colour bar' and the Americans called 'segregation' – stopping black GIs from mixing with whites. The US army tried hard to get the British government to agree to segregation in clubs and pubs used by US troops. After a debate in Parliament on the matter, the British refused. The debate made much of the fact that many soldiers fighting for Britain were not white but soldiers of various races from British **colonies**.

This does not mean the British treated black people as equals. They had a much more subtle form of discrimination, where black people were very seldom likely to rise to become officers, but were allowed to mix freely with whites below a certain level. One of the things that shocked the British about the US system was how open it was in its prejudice.

No prejudice?

In 1944 George Roberts, a West Indian who lived in Liverpool, was refused entrance to a dance hall because of his colour. Roberts had been living in Liverpool for many years and was an engineer in a factory producing ammunition for the war. He was also a volunteer in the Home Guard. Roberts went home and changed into his Home Guard uniform and returned. He was still turned away. He therefore refused to do his Home Guard duties, in protest. When he was prosecuted for this, he was, at first, fined £5. However, he appealed and the judge who heard the appeal cancelled the fine. He said that people who came from any part of the world to fight for Britain should be treated equally under the law.

SOURCE E

As I walked down the road to the postbox, the entire village turned out to watch me. They watched me walk there, post the letter and walk back. They didn't say anything, just watched. They weren't hostile, just curious. I felt just as Dr Livingstone must have felt in the heart of Africa, as the first white man the African people had seen.

From an interview with a West Indian soldier, about his wartime experiences in Bury St Edmunds, Suffolk.

Closing the Casino Club

In 1942 RAF Burtonwood, near Warrington, became one of the largest US airbases in Europe. Warrington was suddenly full of GIs. They brought glamour to Warrington – the actor James Cagney visited the troops, the famous boxer Joe Louis boxed in a local park. Many GIs were black. At the base, black and white GIs were segregated. Black soldiers had lower pay for doing the same work as white soldiers. Their housing was worse and they were given the worst work to do. Off base, there were attempts at segregation, too.

One of the most popular Warrington clubs was the Casino Club, run by Nat Bookbinder. One evening, a group of white GIs objected to a black GI entering the club and told Bookbinder to throw him out. Bookbinder refused. He told the black GI, Herbert Greaves, that he was welcome as long as he could pay the entrance fee and keep to the rules, like everyone else. The US army then wrote to Bookbinder, asking him to ban all coloured people from the club 'in the interests of eliminating trouble that might involve our troops'. Bookbinder refused.

SOURCE F

Black GIs dancing with white women in an English dance hall. Talking about the war, a woman remembered that black GIs were very popular with her friends; they were 'exotic'.

The US army then told GIs not to use the club. The British government had refused to set up a colour bar, (leaving it to the US army to do so) but British and Canadian troops were also told not to go to the Casino. The War Office said this was because of reports of 'overcrowding'. The club emptied and began to lose money. Bookbinder was conscripted into the army and the club was forced to close. Other clubs in Warrington quietly fitted in with the needs of the US army.

Work it out!

1. **a** How does the story about George Roberts show two different British attitudes to black people?
   b Why do you think the British people in Source E behaved as they did?

2. **a** What was the British government's official attitude to discrimination against black people?
   b Why then do you think they therefore banned their troops from the Casino Club?

3. **a** 'The story of the Casino Club illustrates US prejudice and British hypocrisy about black people.' Do you agree?
   b How might the US and British war departments have excused the way they behaved?

Keeping each other going

During the Second World War millions of people that the **Nazis** in Germany called 'undesirables' were shipped off to **concentration camps**. Many of these people were Jews. Some early camps were labour camps, where people were sent to work. Later, the Nazis set up 'death camps' to kill off as many Jews as possible. At best, people were badly housed and badly fed. They shared inadequate toilets and washing facilities, which they could only use at certain times of day. They were forced to work hard, even when ill. For most inmates of the camps, it took all their strength just to survive. Yet those who survived remember some people who worked to remind themselves, and their captors, that they were human beings, not animals.

Terezin: Ghetto and camp

People tried to keep life as normal as possible. At first the town was run by a Council of Jewish Elders who set up lectures and concerts almost every day. Composers such as Viktor Ullmann wrote music. Hans Krasa wrote *Brundibar*, an opera for children, which was performed 55 times in the ghetto, and is still played now. Almost all of the first occupants of Terezin died there or were sent to death camps. It became a camp run by guards, not a ghetto run by Jews. Then the Allies began to advance into German-occupied land. Terezin was the last camp out of their reach, so was filled with Jews moved from other camps.

Terezin

Terezin is about 35 miles (56 kilometres) north of Prague, in Czechoslovakia. It was a small town and fort, walled and self contained. In 1941 the Nazis made it a 'Jewish self-governing town'. This means it became a **ghetto**. Once Jewish people were herded into ghettos, it was just a matter of time before they were taken off to death camps such as Birkenau, part of Auschwitz. From 1941–4 over 150,000 people passed through Terezin. About 35,000 people died there.

SOURCE A

This landscape was painted in Auschwitz, by a prisoner, Bronislaw Czech, in 1942. The commander of the camp, Rudolf Hoess, saw a prisoner, Franciszek Targosz, drawing a picture of a horse and liked it. Targosz persuaded Hoess to set up an art collection and to allow artists to paint pictures to give to important visitors to Auschwitz. This saved the artists from heavy work, which was almost certain to kill them.

This drawing shows prisoners returning from work. They are carrying someone who has died during the day. The drawing was made secretly in Auschwitz on a piece of cardboard and hidden from the guards.

SOURCE B

Women and children

Auschwitz was really a collection of camps, not just one camp. It had a labour camp, a series of factory and farming camps and a death camp. A visitor to Birkenau, the death camp in Auschwitz, can walk around the huts that still stand there. The brick-built huts had an area in the middle where everyone had to stand to be counted. In a few of these areas there are paintings by prisoners on the walls. Men were kept apart from the women and children. In one of the huts in the women's section there are paintings on the walls of a fairy-tale life, obviously painted to amuse the children. While the guards must have known about the wall paintings, there were many other things the women did in secret to try to keep the children's spirits up, such as making toys and presents out of scraps of cloth and wood.

Work it out!

1. **a** Read **Terezin: Ghetto and camp**. How do you think the concerts that were organised there would have helped the Jewish people imprisoned in the ghetto?
   b Auschwitz camp had an orchestra too. It was chosen by the guards and played marches and songs as the work gangs went out to work each morning and returned at night. What sort of effect do you think this orchestra would have had on the people imprisoned in Auschwitz? Explain your answer.

2. Read **Women and children**.
   a Why do you think the women painted the walls of the hut with the fairy-tale pictures?
   b The guards must have known about these pictures. Why might they have left them there?
   c Why do you think the toys and others gifts were made in secret?

3. Compare Source A and Source B.
   a Why were they painted/drawn?
   b How might the other prisoners in Auschwitz have felt about each artist making them? Do you think all the prisoners would have felt the same?

Adolf Eichmann: Nazi on the run

When the Second World War came to an end the full horror of the Nazi treatment of Jews and others they called 'undesirable' became clear. People wanted those who had taken part in the **Holocaust** to be punished. However, it was not that easy. While many Nazis had been rounded up to be brought to trial, many others had escaped in the confusion of the **Allied** advance, some even disguised themselves as **concentration camp** survivors.

Among those who escaped was the man who was in charge of the 'Final Solution' to kill all Jewish people in Nazi-held lands – Adolf Eichmann. David Ben Gurion, the first Prime Minister of the newly created Jewish State of Israel, said, in May 1948, that it was the duty of Jewish survivors to tell their stories and to catch those involved in the Holocaust, especially Eichmann.

The hunt was on. But where was Eichmann?

Adolf Eichmann to Otto Eckmann

Eichmann was captured in 1945, at the end of the war, by US troops. He was put in a Prisoner of War camp, along with many other Nazis. At first, no one realised how involved in the Holocaust he had been. Knowing that the truth would catch up with him sooner or later, he managed to escape from the camp a few weeks after his arrival. He was captured again fairly soon after, as part of the continuing round-up of Nazis. He was put into another camp, but this time he gave his name as Otto Eckmann.

Otto Eckmann to Otto Henninger

As the war trials went on, evidence of Eichmann's role piled up. He realised that there would be searches of the camps to find him. Sooner or later he would be recognised. So he staged another escape, in 1946, this time to the mountains of central Germany. Here he took on the identity of Otto Henninger, working as a chicken farmer. However, while he wanted to stay in Germany, it soon became clear that the widening search made it dangerous to stay where he was. He had to leave the country.

Otto Henninger to Ricardo Klement

Eichmann fled to Italy in 1948. Here, hiding in a monastery, he got himself new identity papers. By 1949 escaped Nazis had formed their own secret movement to help each other escape and were travelling to South America in significant numbers. Eichmann joined them in 1950. He went to live in a small village in the mountains of Argentina. By 1952 he felt safe enough to send instructions for his wife and two sons, left behind in Germany, to join him. They met up in Buenos Aires, where they moved into a poor area of the city and Eichmann found work with a rabbit farmer and then, quite soon after, as a mechanic in the Mercedes Benz car factory there. Soon he was the factory foreman. It was here that the Israeli secret service, Mossad, tracked him down in 1959.

SOURCE A

Eichmann's forged identity papers as Ricardo Klement.

Found!

Mossad agents, led by Zvi Aharoni, first made sure that the man they had found really was Eichmann. They watched him carefully. They took photos of him; even stopping him in the street to ask directions, so that they could take close-up photos from a camera hidden in a briefcase. At last they had enough evidence to be sure that Klement was Eichmann. But what to do next? One of the reasons that the Nazis had hidden out in South America in such numbers was that the various South American governments were sympathetic to them. If Mossad told the Argentine government that they had found Eichmann and wanted to take him back to Israel for trial, the Argentines would have refused. They would not bring him to trial in Argentina, either.

The Mossad agents mapped Eichmann's daily movements. On 11 May 1960, they grabbed him as he got off the bus on his way home from work. They took him to a secret hideout, questioned him and got him to sign a statement saying that he was willing to go back to Israel for trial. They then drugged him and smuggled him out of the country. Once they had him safe in Israel they questioned him thoroughly and then brought him to trial. He was found guilty and executed on 31 May 1962.

Reactions to the capture

When David Ben Gurion announced to the Israeli parliament that Eichmann had been captured, people were stunned, then delighted that he would be brought to trial. The Argentine government complained to the UN that Israel had no right to send agents secretly to Argentina and take someone out of the country without asking the government. Israel's foreign minister, Golda Meier, said that Mossad's action was justified. A UN enquiry was set up to investigate and agreed a compromise: Israel apologised and promised not to do this sort of thing again, but Argentina did not demand the return of Eichmann.

Work it out!

How might the following people have reacted to the capture of Eichmann:

- a Nazi in hiding in Brazil
- an Auschwitz survivor
- an Allied soldier who had seen the death camps
- Eichmann's wife, in Argentina
- a German farmer?

The swinging 60s

The 1960s was a time when Britain, especially London, exploded into a riot of colour and noise. London was seen as a worldwide focus for youth fashion, music and dance. The area around Carnaby Street and the King's Road were full of 'boutiques' selling fashionable clothes that drew people not only from England, but from all over the world, especially young people. In 1965 the American singer Roger Miller sang a song that began *'England swings like a pendulum do...'* the American Magazine *Time* picked up the idea, featuring London on its cover for April 1966 under the headline *London: the Swinging City*.

New!

Following the many years of saving and re-using during and after the Second World War, the 60s became a time when people wanted to indulge in colourful clothes and to 'enjoy it today, sling it tomorrow'. The trendiest clothes and furniture were cheap and disposable. The most fashionable clothes were often badly made from new **synthetic** fibres. They did not last long, but that was no longer important. They were cheap. Besides, soon people would be wearing totally different styles anyway. Suddenly everyone, not just the rich, could afford to follow fashion. Almost anyone could try to shape fashion, too. Young designers did not have to join long-established firms and design what they were told. They could take a risk, set up their own company and design what they wanted. Many tried and failed. A few were a huge success.

Mary Quant started the trend for mini skirts and dresses, which could be taken to extreme lengths!

Mary Quant

Mary Quant was one of the first young designers to launch the 60s fashion boom. She opened her shop, Bazaar, in 1955. Her most famous design was the short mini skirt, which was worn shorter and shorter. In 1958 the first minis caused shock by being two inches above the knee. By 1965 they were nearly six inches above the knee, and dry-cleaners were pricing skirt cleaning by the inch! In a later interview about the 60s, Mary Quant said: *'There was simply nothing for young people when I started. The older generation wanted to go back to the pre-war way; we wanted to go forward, to do something new. I loved using new material like PVC and mixing old-fashioned men's suit material with loads of lace. I just made things for friends at first. It was a Chelsea thing: fashion people, furniture designers, artists, musicians and playwrights, we all hung out together and influenced each other.'*

SOURCE A

Beatlemania

London may have become the fashion capital of the world in the 1960s, but it was in Liverpool that the music sensation of the decade exploded. All over Britain young people were forming rock and roll groups, imitating the music craze from the USA and trying to break into the big time. One group of boys from Liverpool succeeded beyond their wildest dreams – the Beatles.

The Beatles were one of the first groups to win worldwide fame and to attract hordes of screaming fans wherever they went. In keeping with the 60s emphasis on new things, they wrote their own words and music, rather than playing hit songs by US groups. For the first time a British group became a hit in the USA, rather than the other way round. On their US tour in October 1964 the Beatles played in 25 cities over 32 days. They played to half a million people and flew 40,000 miles (64,000 kilometres). It was the biggest tour of any group ever at that time.

Almost famous?

The first Beatles were John Lennon, Paul McCartney, George Harrison, and Stuart Sutcliffe. They were later joined by a drummer called Pete Best. Who were Sutcliffe and Best? Stuart Sutcliffe was an art college friend of John Lennon, who left the group to follow his artistic career and died in 1962. Pete Best stayed with the group for longer and, while he was with the group, was the most popular of them all. He left the group in September 1962, to be replaced by Ringo Starr, who joined the group from another band, Rory Storm and the Hurricanes. The Beatles already had many fans all over Merseyside, who reacted badly to Best leaving. The Beatles new manager, Brian Epstein, said Best wanted to go. Best himself wrote, in 1963: *'Just before the first release I was told I would have to leave the group. The news came as a big surprise to me as I had no hint that it would happen and didn't even have the opportunity of discussing it with the rest of the group.'* Feeling ran so high that in the Beatles' first appearance with Ringo Starr, Pete Best fans began a fight, which ended up involving the whole club, and George Harrison came out with a black eye! Immediately after Best left the Beatles made their first record, 'Love Me Do', and began their rapid rise to stardom.

SOURCE B

A photograph of the Beatles taken when Pete Best was a member.

Motorway madness

In the 60s Britain's road network expanded rapidly and the first motorways were built. By 1969 there were 600 miles (over 900 kilometres) of motorway and many 'ring roads' to direct the traffic around major towns. In 1964 the minister for transport, Ernest Marples announced: *towns of the future must be rebuilt to come to terms with the motor vehicle.* Cars became affordable in the same way as fashion and household goods, like washing machines. In 1960 there were 5.6 million cars on Britain's roads. In 1969 there were 11.5 million. Teenagers and young people who could not afford cars could afford the scooters that were becoming popular. People could get around far more easily and cheaply than ever before.

A different sort of mini. The mini car was first produced in August 1959 and became the car of the 60s. It cost £497. (A Rover 2000 cost £1298.) Many people painted their minis with the Union Jack flag, flowers or simply bright swirls of colour.

SOURCE C

Mods and rockers

In the mid 1960s the transport revolution took an unexpected twist. Followers of two different fashion and music styles, calling themselves 'mods' and 'rockers' took off on scooters and motorbikes to seaside resorts such as Brighton, Hastings and Clacton in large gangs over weekends and Bank Holidays. It became common for these gangs to meet and fight. There were many injuries and some deaths.

Rules of the road

More cars on the roads meant more rules. The first traffic wardens appeared in London in 1960. They issued 344 parking tickets on their first day's work. MOT tests, to check that cars were safe, were introduced in 1961. In 1967, after a steep rise in deaths on the road due to drunk driving, police were given the first 'breathalyser' machines to detect drunk drivers. Deaths on the road dropped to a quarter of their previous rate within months of breathalysers coming into use.

40

The B side of the 60s?

For many people the 60s were an exciting and profitable time. Not everyone was so lucky. Coalmines were shutting, throwing whole villages out of work. Government schemes for re-developing areas of Britain led to compulsory purchase orders being placed on many homes in run down areas. This meant that local councils could choose a run down area and make the people who lived there sell their homes to the council for a price set by the council. Their homes were then pulled down and replaced with brand new developments. There was not always a place in these new developments for the people who had been turned out of their homes. They added to the growing numbers of homeless in the country.

Work it out!

1. Were the 60s a good time?

   Choose one aspect covered here (for instance the rise in car ownership) and show how it had both good and bad sides.

> The 60s were great. My Mum lived in London and she remembers all the clothes and having money to spend from her first job and how exciting it all was.

> The 60s were awful. My Dad's family in London had their house compulsorily purchased and two of them who worked on the railways lost their jobs.

> The 60s were awful. My uncle lived in Wales and his coalmine had closed and he never got another job. It was awful in those pit villages.

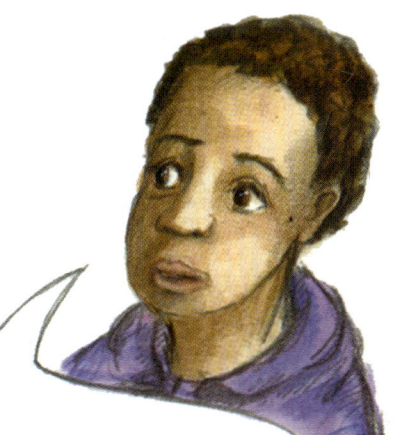

Warfare in the twentieth century

At the turn of the century Britain was at war with the Boers of South Africa. In the Boer War (1899–1902) a major part was played by the cavalry and several towns found themselves under siege from enemy forces. Soon, however, warfare was to change dramatically.

A new kind of warfare?

When the First World War broke out in August 1914, British men, and men from many parts of the empire, rushed to join the army. Few of them knew what they were letting themselves in for. The Boer War had not been a major conflict and Britain had lost just 28,000 men in the whole war. (There were over 20,000 men killed in one single day at the Battle of the Somme in 1916.) The last major war (the Crimean War) had been in the mid-nineteenth century, so none of the million young men who volunteered in 1914 knew what warfare was really like.

Instead they found themselves caught up in a huge wave of patriotism. Posters in all the main towns encouraged men to 'do their bit' for the country. Those who did not join up were made to feel that they were letting Britain down. Sometimes women handed out white feathers as a sign of cowardice. But most men did not need encouragement. Many came from boring, mundane jobs and saw the war as a chance for adventure. They wanted to join up – and fast. The war, they were told, would be 'over by Christmas'.

Source A

Men queuing outside a recruiting office at the beginning of the war.

The generals in the army believed that it would be a short and glorious war. However Lord Kitchener, the Minister for War, did tell the government he would need a million men. He thought the fighting would last much longer than four months, probably for years. Most people thought the First World War would be fought like all previous wars. Men would charge at the enemy, either on horseback with their swords flashing, or running with their bayonets attached to their rifles. The winners would be those who held their nerve and did not run away.

Shells for the artillery, in a First World War munitions factory.

Stalemate

The First World War did not finish by Christmas. It dragged on for more than four years and cost more than seven million lives. The reason for this was that technological advances had produced weapons which meant that the traditional warfare with cavalry and infantry charges usually produced little more than huge numbers of casualties for the attacking side. In September 1914 both sides had dug trenches from the Channel coast to Switzerland to protect themselves. This 600 kilometre stretch became known as the Western Front. For four years each side tried to cross **No Man's Land** to attack the enemy. What stopped them was the newly-developed machine gun, which could fire up to sixteen bullets a second. As men obeyed their generals' orders to 'go over the top' and attack enemy trenches, some were killed even before they had finished climbing out of their own trench. The result was **stalemate** as neither side was able to advance or gain superiority over the other.

New weapons

Scientists and engineers tried to develop new weapons to break the stalemate of the trenches. Huge artillery guns were used to bombard enemy trenches before an attack, but often the bombardment did little more than churn up No Man's Land and tangle the barbed wire making it even harder to cross. In April 1915, the Germans fired poisonous gas into enemy trenches. Soon, however, the use of gas masks restricted the effectiveness of this new weapon. In April 1916 the British launched a new weapon – the tank. Fifty tanks were used in the Battle of the Somme. But they all broke down. Although the tank was more effective in battles later in the war, its day was still to come. The same was true of the airplane, although by the end of the war both sides were able to carry out air bombing raids on enemy cities.

Blitzkrieg

By the time that the Second World War (1939–45) broke out weapons had become so advanced that the static warfare of 1914–18 could not be repeated. By 1939 tanks could easily crash through barbed wire and enemy trenches. The development of aircraft meant that soldiers in trenches would simply be sitting ducks. The new tactic, first used by the Germans in their attack on Poland in September 1939, was 'Blitzkrieg'. This involved surprise attacks on the enemy using artillery and dive bombers, followed by the advance of tanks and paratroopers and then the infantry foot soldiers. Using this method Hitler was able to conquer most of Western Europe in the first year of the war.

The bombing raids

As the war developed, aircraft were used to attack enemy cities. In the autumn of 1940 the Germans decided to launch a massive bombing raid on Britain's cities. There had been some bombing in the First World War, but Hitler's **Blitz** was on a far bigger scale. By 1941 43,000 British civilians had been killed and 2 million made homeless. From 1942 the Allies bombed German cities. The effect of these bombing raids was horrific. For example, on 13 February 1945 up to 135,000 people were killed in a bombing raid on Dresden, which destroyed 80 per cent of the city.

SOURCE C

The London docks after the first mass raid on London by German bombers in September 1940.

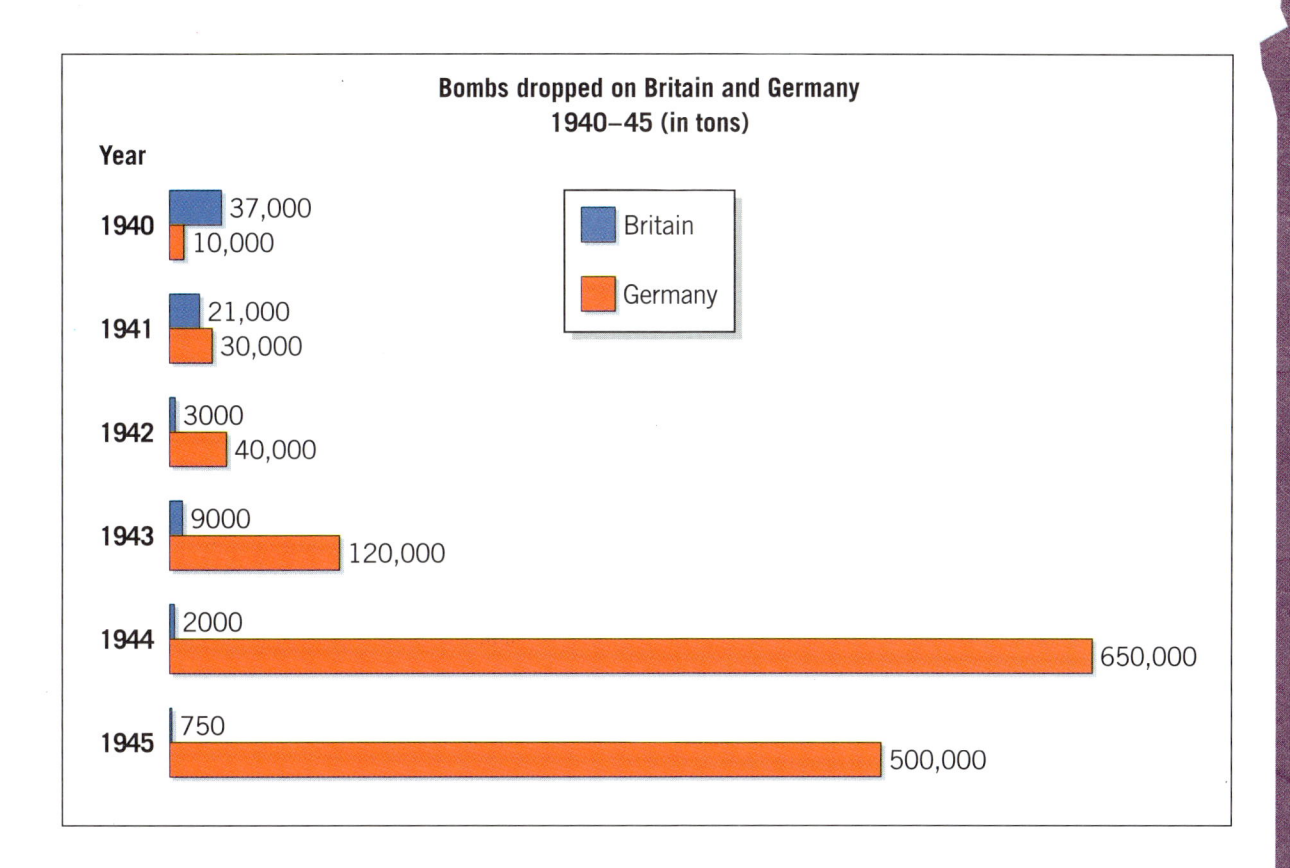

**Bombs dropped on Britain and Germany
1940–45 (in tons)**

Year	Britain	Germany
1940	37,000	10,000
1941	21,000	30,000
1942	3000	40,000
1943	9000	120,000
1944	2000	650,000
1945	750	500,000

The most significant development was not the improved aircraft, but the type of bombs they dropped. In Dresden thousands of people were killed because incendiary bombs had been dropped. These were designed to start fires. As the city blazed people fainted through lack of oxygen and were then burned to death.

Invisible death

In 1945 came the most important development in the history of warfare – the atomic bomb. The Japanese refused to surrender throughout July 1945. On 6 August the Americans dropped an atomic bomb on the city of Hiroshima. Almost 80,000 Japanese men, women and children died instantly. The atomic bomb carried with it a deadly after effect. Radiation sickness followed the initial explosion, causing many more deaths than the bomb itself. A second bomb was dropped three days later on Nagasaki causing around 40,000 deaths, which were later matched by deaths from the after effects. Even today the grandchildren of the survivors of Hiroshima and Nagasaki can suffer birth defects. It seemed that the ultimate weapon of war had been developed.

The Cold War

The development of the atomic bomb was followed by that of the more powerful hydrogen bomb in 1952. Then scientists worked out how to attach these bombs to unmanned rockets (Intercontinental Ballistic Missiles) that could travel thousands of kilometres to reach their target. They even developed ways to fire them from submarines under the sea! Today's nuclear weapons have over 100 times the destructive power of the first bombs dropped on Hiroshima and Nagasaki.

FLASHPOINTS IN THE COLD WAR

1946–8 Pro-communist governments established in Eastern Europe

1947 Truman Doctrine and Marshall Plan. USA pledges to help countries 'maintain their freedoms'

1948 Berlin Airlift. USA, Britain and France act to stop Soviet Union taking control of Berlin

1949 North Atlantic Treaty Organisation (NATO) formed to protect anti-communist countries

1955 The Soviet Union forms the Warsaw Pact to oppose NATO

1950 Korean War. USA and Soviet Union support different sides

1956 Hungarian Revolt. Soviet Union crushes opposition to its influence in Hungary

1961 Soviet Union builds Berlin Wall

1962 Cuban Missile Crisis. Soviet Union tries to install nuclear missiles in Cuba (within range of USA)

1965-73 Vietnam War. USA and Soviet Union support different sides

1968 Czechoslovakia. Soviet Union crushes opposition to its influence in Czechoslovakia

1979 Soviet troops invade Afghanistan to support its communist government.

SOURCE D

A cartoon published in 1962 showing President Kennedy of the USA and Chairman Khrushchev of the Soviet Union fighting over the issue of missiles in Cuba.

One reason for the development of weapons after the Second World War was the **Cold War** between the USA and the Soviet Union after 1945. An 'arms race' began between the two sides. Each side tried to ensure that it had the latest weapons and, if possible, more than its opponent in order to have the advantage if fighting broke out. Although there were times when the two sides came close to war, the Cold War remained one of propaganda and words rather than direct action. Both the USA and the Soviet Union knew that if they ever used nuclear weapons then they might be responsible for terrible destruction around the world. They each had the capacity to destroy each other hundreds of times over. Even though weapons of almost unimaginable power now exist, no one has ever used them – or wants to be the first to do so!

Vietnam

So, in any fighting since 1945 it has not been atomic or nuclear weapons which have been used to bring victory. Instead, the airplane has continued to be the main attack weapon. Perhaps the best known of the conflicts since the Second World War occurred during the 1960s and 1970s when the USA tried to prevent communist fighters from taking over the government of South Vietnam. During the war the USA dropped more bombs on Vietnam than were dropped in the entire Second World War. They also used their planes to drop chemicals, such as napalm and Agent Orange, to destroy the forest that was the protection for the communist Vietcong. Despite their huge superiority in weapons, the Americans could not win this war.

Source E

A low flying US bomber casts its shadow over a bridge in North Vietnam destroyed by US bombing.

The jungle **terrain** meant their enemy's **guerrilla** tactics proved much more effective. Although developments in technology had led to weapons no one could have dreamed of in 1900, it was still possible for determined fighters using traditional tactics to defeat one of the world's strongest nations.

War in the 1990s

As the twentieth century came to a close the importance of air power was emphasised in the Gulf War (1991). The **United Nations** agreed to take action against Saddam Hussein of Iraq for invading neighbouring Kuwait. In the short war that followed, the United Nations'

Source F

A woman in the centre of Grozny following Russian bombing in 1999.

forces used aircraft to knock out thousands of Iraqi tanks. The aircraft also had laser-guided bombs to ensure a greater degree of accuracy in their bombing. Saddam Hussein was forced to withdraw from Kuwait and the United Nations won a victory with very few casualties to its forces.

Bombing was also a major part of the campaign waged against Serbia by members of the North Atlantic Treaty Organisation (NATO). The Serbian leader, Slobodan Milosevic, tried to absorb the province of Kosovo into Serbia. The Kosovans resisted this move and Serbian attacks on the Kosovan people lead to NATO launching air attacks on Serbia in March 1999. There followed a 79 day air-campaign during which NATO planes made 22,000 attacks on Serbia. NATO also threatened to send ground troops into Serbia. Eventually Slobodan Milosevic was forced to back down.

The year 2000 has also seen Russian troops involved in heavy fighting. In 1991 the Russian province of Chechnya declared its independence from Russia. In 1994 Russian forces invaded Chechnya and severely damaged its capital, Grozny. Peace was made in 1996, but fighting broke out again in November 1999 when Russian planes and artillery bombarded Grozny and once again the city was almost totally destroyed.

Source G

During its air campaign NATO said that its planes had hit hundreds of Serbian tanks and other military vehicles. The Serbian army said that only 13 tanks were destroyed. NATO's supreme commander for Europe, General Wesley Clark, acknowledged that only 26 tank wreckages had been found, but said that the Serbs had removed the rest. 'It is just basic military doctrine to clean up the battlefield after an engagement' he said.

An extract from a news website on 16 September 1999.

Work it out!

1 a What weapons are mentioned in this unit?

  b Would you say that the weapons used at the end of the twentieth century were:

   the same as
   similar to
   completely different to

   those used at the beginning of the century? Give as many reasons as you can for your answer.

2 Do you agree that the invention of the atomic bomb changed the way wars are fought? Explain your answer.

3 'Technological advances have meant that we can never have wars like the First and Second World Wars again.' How far do you agree with this statement?

4 Research:

  a Use the Internet or back copies of newspapers to find out how many countries are experiencing fighting at the moment.

  b How similar is that warfare to the fighting in the First World War?

Controlling the hearts and minds of the people: propaganda in the twentieth century

Perhaps more than at any other time in our history, the twentieth century was a time when there was an almost constant attempt to influence the way people thought. Advanced methods of communication, such as radio, television and the internet bombarded people with messages about such things as the best clothes to wear and what sort of lifestyle they should follow to be seen to be fashionable. If someone asked you to write down what you would buy if you had unlimited amounts of money, you would almost certainly choose a house, a car and clothes based on what you think 'rich' and 'cool' people should have. Unless you are already 'rich' and 'cool' yourself, that image will have come to you largely from advertising. Companies selling certain goods want you to think that what they have is what you want. That is the purpose of advertising.

Propaganda

Propaganda is the use of information to influence the way that people think. Advertising is a form of propaganda. Such tactics are not restricted just to advertising, however. Governments throughout history have used propaganda to help them rule effectively.

Look at the poster in Source A. This was issued by the British government at the start of the First World War (1914–18). Why do you think it was issued? There are numerous clues in the picture. Let us look at how people are portrayed:

1 The British soldier
He is seen helpless and wounded, reaching up to beg for water.

2 The German nurse
She has some water, but instead of giving it to the soldier, she tips it on the ground in front of him! Look at the way she is standing. She has a defiant pose and is obviously enjoying being cruel.

3 The German soldiers
In the background are two German soldiers. They look as if they are enjoying the nurse's cruelty. Perhaps they have ordered her to be cruel. They also look rather silly, especially compared to the more realistic portrayal of the British soldier.

4 The message
By now you will have got the idea of what the government was trying to say. But in case it was not obvious to people at the time, the British government added some emotive language to explain the cartoon. Notice the use of the word 'cries' and the fact that the behaviour of the nurse is something that 'no woman in Britain' would do. So, overall we have a message that Germans behave in an unacceptable way and are obviously bad people.

Why would the British government want to make people think that?

SOURCE A

RED CROSS OR IRON CROSS?

WOUNDED AND A PRISONER
OUR SOLDIER CRIES FOR WATER.

THE GERMAN "SISTER"
POURS IT ON THE GROUND BEFORE HIS EYES.

THERE IS NO WOMAN IN BRITAIN
WHO WOULD DO IT.

THERE IS NO WOMAN IN BRITAIN
WHO WILL FORGET IT.

THE DANGERFIELD PRINTING CO. LTD. LONDON.

A poster issued by the British government at the beginning of the First World War.

Now look at Source B. This concerns the way that the German invasion of Belgium in 1914 was reported in the newspapers. The extracts are printed in the order in which they appeared in 1914. In August the Germans had sent an army of over one million men into Belgium on its way to France. Although the Belgians put up fierce resistance (particularly in trying to stop the Germans from capturing Antwerp) they were soon defeated. Early in August Britain and France declared war on Germany. Before the war Italy had been an ally of Germany. However, Italy did not join in the war until May 1915 – and then on the side of Britain and France.

Work it out!

1. Explain briefly how the story of the German behaviour has changed between Extract 1 and Extract 4.
2. Explain how the four accounts are connected (other than that they are covering the same story!).
3. a What do you notice about the way the use of language is different in Extract 4 to the other sources?
   b Why do you think this is?
4. Explain whether you agree or disagree with each of these statements:
   a Extract 1 is obviously true, because the Germans were there and would know what happened.
   b All the extracts are giving a reliable account of what happened. They are probably describing different events.
   c None of the extracts can be believed. They are all examples of propaganda.

Source B

Extract 1

When the fall of Antwerp became known, the church bells were rung in Koln and all over Germany.

Written in the German newspaper *Kolnische Zeitung*, published in Koln (Cologne).

Extract 2

According to the *Kolnische Zeitung* the clergy at Antwerp were compelled to ring the church bells when the town was captured.

Written in the French newspaper, *Le Matin*.

Extract 3

According to what the British newspaper *The Times* has heard from Cologne, via Paris, the unfortunate Belgian priests who refused to ring the church bells when Antwerp was taken, have been sentenced to hard labour.

Written in the Italian newspaper *Corriere della Sera*.

Extract 4

According to information which has reached *Corriere della Sera* from Cologne, via London, it is confirmed that the barbaric conquerors of Antwerp punished the unfortunate Belgian priests for their heroic refusal to ring the church bells by hanging them as living clappers to the bells with their heads down.

Written in *Le Matin*.

SOURCE C

During the Second World War, the British government did not allow newspapers to publish pictures showing the widespread destruction caused by German bombing. Why do you think the government allowed this picture to be published in a daily newspaper?

The Second World War

In both the First World War and the Second World War, the British Government controlled the media, namely newspapers and newsreels and the radio. This was considered necessary to keep up the morale of the people. After all, stories of defeats, details of high casualties, or mass destruction by air raids would be bound to upset people. What the Government had to do was keep the people determined to continue the war and to persuade men to go to fight. It had to persuade the civilian population to put up with the hardships that war brought – such as food shortages and damage from enemy bombing. It also had to raise morale by suggesting ways that civilians could help the war effort and convincing them the Government was in control.

The Vietnam War

An extremely good example of why governments want to control information in a war can be seen from the US involvement in the Vietnam War (1964–75). This was the first 'media war'. Every television station and newspaper in the USA had journalists near or in the war zone. Pictures and accounts of what was happening arrived regularly in the homes of the American people. They were horrified by what they saw; the real images of war are not the same as those of a Hollywood film. It was this exposure to the realities of war which led to a massive campaign against the war. This helped to persuade the government to pull its troops out of Vietnam. The US government had not been able to control the flow of information, and had lost the support of the American people for the war.

Peacetime, too

Most people would accept that propaganda is necessary during wartime, but might not be so keen to see it used in peacetime. Yet there are many examples of the use of propaganda to keep a government in power by increasing its popularity.

The Nazi government in Germany was highly effective in using information to influence its peoples' thoughts. Hitler appointed Joseph Goebbels as his Minister of Propaganda and he set about controlling all forms of media. No newspaper, film, poster or book could be published without first getting his ministry's approval. Only the works of artists approved of by the Nazis were allowed to be shown to the public. Books that were not approved of were publicly burnt. To ensure that all future generations of Germans would believe in the ideals of the Nazis, education and the curriculum were strictly controlled.

Source E

In the next issue of your paper there must be a lead article, featured as prominently as possible, in which a decision of the Führer, no matter what it will be, will be discussed as the only correct one for Germany.

Instructions issued to the German press by the Ministry of Propaganda two days before the outbreak of the Second World War.

Source D

The headline from a German newspaper in the summer of 1938. At the time the Germans were trying to take over the part of Czechoslovakia called the Sudetenland. They said that the Germans who were living there were being mistreated by the local Czechs.

PREGNANT SUDETEN GERMAN MOTHER PUSHED OFF BICYCLE BY CZECH SUB-HUMAN IN OSTRAVIA

Source F

A Soviet painting showing Lenin and Stalin working together. It was painted under the orders of Stalin.

After the death of the Soviet leader Lenin in 1924, there was a power struggle for control of the country. Eventually Stalin won control and his main rival, Trotsky was expelled. Stalin set about rewriting history. Since most Soviet citizens saw Lenin as the 'Father of the Revolution', Stalin portrayed himself as Lenin's closest friend. This had not been the case when Lenin had been alive. Lenin had actually warned that Stalin would not make a good leader and should not be allowed to have power. Stalin managed to keep this quiet and had such strong control over Soviet society that soon people believed that he was Lenin's choice as ruler. The Soviets had a very apt saying: 'Who controls the past controls the future.'

Source G

The process of continuous alteration of past copies was applied not only to newspapers, but to books, periodicals, pamphlets, posters, leaflets, films, sound tracks, cartoons, photographs – to every kind of literature or documentation which might conceivably hold any political or ideological significance. Day by day, almost minute by minute the past was brought up to date.

In this way every prediction made by the Party could be shown by documentary evidence to have been correct: nor was any item of news, or any opinion, which was in conflict with the present thinking, ever allowed to remain on record.

An extract from the book *1984*, written by the Englishman George Orwell in 1949. The main character, Winston Smith, works for the Ministry of Truth and his job is to change what past newspapers said to reflect what the present Party government wanted to believe about the past. The book portrays life as Orwell imagined it might be in 1984.

Work it out!

1. **a** Why did the US government fail to control the flow of information about the Vietnam War?
   b Do you think this means that governments can no longer use propaganda during wartime? Explain your answer.

2. What do you think we can learn about the use of propaganda from Sources D, E and F? Explain your answer.

3. **a** What is meant by the phrase: 'He who controls the past, controls the future'?
   b Do you think George Orwell would have agreed with this view?

4. 'Governments have no right to use propaganda – at least not in peacetime'. Explain whether you agree with this view. (Hint: You might want to consider things like campaigns against drink driving before you make your mind up!)

Taking time out

In 1900 the average working week was over 52 hours a week. By 1939, this had fallen to 48 hours and by 1980, many workers were working less than 39 hours a week. As the century came to a close this figure had fallen to 38 hours. Less time working meant more free time.

As well as working shorter hours, workers began to be given paid holiday time. In 1939, the average worker received one week's paid holiday. In the 1950s this rose to two weeks and by 2000 it was over three weeks. People also experienced an increase in the value of their wages – their money could buy more. So, people had more time to enjoy themselves and more money to spend on their leisure time.

Trips to the seaside

The development of the railways in the nineteenth century provided a cheap and quick means of travel. For the first time many people living in inland Britain took seaside holidays. From the 1870s resorts such as Blackpool, Brighton, Bridlington and Southend began to attract large numbers of visitors, especially on Bank Holiday weekends. Many families went back to the same boarding house, in the same week, every year. A seaside holiday became a traditional break. Then there was a new development – the holiday camp. Billy Butlin opened his first holiday camp at Skegness in 1937. He charged £4 a week 'all-inclusive'. 10,000 people stayed there in the first year that the holiday camp was opened.

This is how long these people would have to work to buy the items shown			
	1900	2000	
Farmworker Police constable Fitter	35 minutes 21 minutes 11 minutes	10 minutes 5 minutes 5.5 minutes	
Farmworker Police constable Fitter	2 hours 35 minutes 1 hour 35 minutes 51 minutes	35 minutes 17 minutes 18 minutes	
Farmworker Police constable Fitter	1 hours 45 minutes 1 hour 5 minutes 35 minutes	5 hours 2 hours 30 minutes 2 hours 36 minutes	
Farmworker Police constable Fitter	13 weeks 2 days 8 weeks 1 day 4 weeks 2 days	4 days 5 hours 2 days 2 hours 2 days 3 hours	

SOURCE A

A re-enactment of a Civil War battle.

Not just the seaside

The countryside was also a holiday attraction now that more and more people began to have cars. In 1930 the Youth Hostel Association (YHA) was formed. It was aimed, primarily, at cyclists who wished to travel around the country at reasonable rates. Cycling was considered a very healthy pursuit, both for the body and mind. Many people took up fell (hill) walking. National Parks attracted a large number of visitors, especially the Lake District. As more people visited the countryside, many began to join organisations such as the National Trust, founded to preserve Britain's countryside, historic buildings and gardens. Today, enjoying the history of Britain is a major leisure pursuit. Historical sites such as the Tower of London or Hadrian's Wall receive millions of visitors each year. Historical re-enactments of Civil War battles, for example, are very popular.

Rambling has become increasingly popular. In 2000 a move to introduce 'freedom to roam' over four million acres of countryside in Britain was under debate in the House of Commons.

By the 50s and 60s caravan holidays were hugely popular. Holiday-makers all over Britain stopped at cheap and reliable sites organised by the Caravan Club. People could see more and more of their own country.

Holidaying abroad

In the same way that the development of rail travel boosted seaside holidays in Britain, developments in air travel led to huge numbers of Britons holidaying abroad. Until the 1960s only the wealthy could afford such holidays. Then holiday companies began offering 'package holidays' which included travel and accommodation all pre-arranged as a block booking by the company. These holidays were very much cheaper than any travel abroad had been before. People who had never been abroad could now go to Spain, Corfu, Greece, the Canaries and many other 'hot spots' where the locals were rapidly building high-rise cheap hotels to accommodate all these new holiday makers.

The number of people going abroad increased dramatically.

Source B

There were two million travellers in 1951; in 1980 there were eight million.

The motor car

Early car users in Britain could only drive at 4mph and had to have a person walking in front of them waving a red flag to warn other travellers that a car was coming. In 1896 the government repealed the Red Flag Act and to celebrate, 40 car drivers set off from London to Brighton, although only fourteen made it to the end. From then on the car developed into the main form of transport in Britain.

The car's main advantage is that drivers are not restricted to certain routes and times as are the travellers using public transport. Nowadays petrol is relatively cheap, cars are easy to maintain and most people can afford to buy one.

However, 100 years ago cars were very expensive to buy and run. Punctures and damaged wheels were frequent, often the result of badly maintained and unsuitable roads. These first cars were hand built by manufacturers such as Herbert Austin, C S Rolls and F H Royce. By 1914 there were 130,000 cars on the roads. Henry Ford, a US car manufacturer, introduced the production line in 1913. Each worker put on a specific part of the car, which moved along a conveyor belt from worker to worker. This was much quicker, and therefore cheaper, than one or two men making the whole car. Ford's philosophy was simple. 'It will be so low in price that any man making a good salary will be able to own one.'

British car manufacturers were quick to copy Ford's methods. By 1938 there were just under two million cars on the road and nearly half a million lorries and vans. As the number of cars increased on Britain's roads it became clear that better roads and more rules to make driving safer were needed.

Some rules of the road

1924	White lines on roads
1926	First traffic lights
1934	First 'cat's-eyes'
1935	Highway Code and driving test
1935	Belisha crossings
1952	Zebra crossings
1965	Motorway speed limit 70 mph
1967	Law against drinking and driving
1982	Front seat belts compulsory
1991	Seat belts compulsory for all seats

Better roads?

The government spent a lot of money improving the roads. To begin with money was spent on improving the surface of roads, but as more and more vehicles appeared, more roads were built. The government built the first motorway (bypassing Preston) in 1958. Since then a wide network of motorways has criss-crossed Britain. The advantages of the motorways were immediately apparent: cars and lorries could travel at faster, consistent speeds without the delays and dangers of numerous crossings and the hazards of pedestrians, tractors, bicycles and learner drivers – all of which are prohibited from going on a motorway. Motorways also take heavy traffic away from towns and villages, as do the network of connecting ring-roads, or bypasses round hundreds of towns and cities.

Accidents

During the twentieth century more than 400,000 people were killed on British roads. Motorways may have made it easier to travel further, faster, but when accidents occur the result is often multi-vehicle 'pile-ups' with large numbers of casualties.

Governments have passed various laws to try to bring down the death toll on roads.

The number killed by the motor car in Britain since 1930

1930 to 1939	69,824
1940 to 1949	61,401
1950 to 1959	54,001
1960 to 1969	72,760
1970 to 1979	69,983
1980 to 1989	54,931
1990 to 1998	35,717

Source C

A traffic jam on the M25 in 1999.

Perhaps the most important of these was the 'no drinking and driving laws' in 1967. Other measures, such as 'traffic calming' schemes and the use of cameras to enforce the speed limits have also helped reduce the number of deaths.

Congestion and pollution

The massive increase in car ownership (almost two out of every three families now has a car) means that, despite increased road building, congestion and the traffic jams continue to grow. In 1985 there were 20 million vehicles on the road, and by 1998 the number of cars alone had reached 22 million. 'Rush hour' in most big cities is a time of long delays, with thousands who drive to and from work caught in traffic jams. Air pollution from car exhausts has led to an increase in health problems (Britain now has 3.5 million asthma sufferers). Noise pollution is also becoming an increasing problem.

Ring roads led to the development of huge retail parks outside towns. These overcame the problems of city centre congestion and parking. But, because these huge shops can sell goods more cheaply than smaller, city centre shops, many city centres are becoming run down and derelict.

Benefits

However, the car has helped create millions of jobs making and manufacturing cars and in related industries, such as road construction, and glass and rubber manufacturing. Workers no longer have to live in the town where they work or even near a railway station to commute to work. There are no limits to travel, with cross-channel ferries and the channel tunnel making the continent as accessible as anywhere in Britain.

The media

Although the twentieth century saw a rapid growth in travel, perhaps the most significant impact on people's leisure time came from the invention of radio, film, and television.

Radio and film

The British Broadcasting Company (BBC) was set up in 1922. Soon it was broadcasting news, plays, talks and music to millions of listeners. In 1922 there were 8000 radio licence holders in Britain. In 1927, this had risen to 2,300,000 and by 1939, it was 8,900,000.

But there was still plenty of entertainment outside the home. In the 1920s dance halls were extremely popular, with ragtime and jazz all the rage. However, their popularity declined in the face of competition from the cinema. Huge numbers of people went to see stars such as Charlie Chaplin and Rudolph Valentino. To begin with the films were silent, but the advent of the 'talkie' allowed for more complicated and realistic plots. After the Second World War, the numbers of people going to see films declined, resulting in the closure of many cinemas. However, since the mid 1980s, attendances at cinemas has increased, with huge multi-screen complexes being opened.

Home cinema?

In 1924, John Logie Baird invented the television. The first televisions were very expensive, and there was only one transmitter in London. All transmissions stopped during the Second World War, but after the war television ownership took off. By 1959, 70 per cent of British households had a TV set. Many people bought a black and white set for Queen Elizabeth II's coronation in 1953. Television came to dominate people's lives. The world seems to have shrunk as live pictures of news or sporting events are transmitted worldwide by satellite.

Initially, people had very limited choice as to what they watched. Until 1957 there was only the BBC. By 1986, the choice had grown to four channels. The advent of satellite and digital television has meant that people now have a much wider choice with dozens of channels offering specialist viewing in sport, films or news. There are even channels dedicated to shopping, as this has become a leisure pursuit in itself.

Source D

Neil Armstrong and Buzz Aldrin plant the US flag on the moon on 20 July 1969. This event was witnessed by millions of people around the world on their TV screens.

The computer

The fastest growing area of leisure in the years since 1990 has been the world of computers. More and more parents are buying PCs to help their children with school work, and computer games are popular with all ages. The game industries are now worth tens of billions of pounds each year. More people are using the Internet, too. People of all ages now use the 'net' to buy goods or find out information; there are very few organisations that do not have a Web site.

Popular music

In 1957 the arrival of Bill Haley and the Comets signalled a new musical form, rock and roll. Since then, 'pop' has dominated the music market. There have been many types of popular music: from rock, soul, and disco, to psychedelic, progressive, punk, futuristic, ska, reggae, new-romantic, gothic, grunge, hip-hop, rap and rave, to name but a few.

It is not just the music that has changed. Forty years ago people bought vinyl records and played them on a record player. Today almost all records are on compact disc (CD) or minidisc. In a few years time, much of the music we listen to will come to us via the Internet.

SOURCE E

Liam and Noel Gallagher from the popular 1990s band, Oasis. The band is heavily influenced by the music of the 1960s.

Work it out!

1. 'The motor car revolutionised twentieth-century life?' Do you agree with this statement?

2. In what ways has television had an impact on the lives of ordinary people?

3. Shopping is now a leisure pursuit. Why do you think previous generations would be surprised that people would spend so much of their time shopping?

4. Why do computers and the Internet now take up so much leisure time?

5. You are to help design an exhibition called 'Leisure in the twentieth century'.
   a. Choose five items to go in your exhibition. Explain why you have chosen them.
   b. Choose five pictures/photographs to go into your exhibition. Explain why you have chosen them.

6. Write a brief passage giving your thoughts on people's leisure habits.